FINDING FAITH

What people are saying about *Finding Faith*

Sharon Gallagher has given us a true gift. In her intelligent, sensitive, and artfully expressive way she tells us stories about diverse people from radically different backgrounds who share one thing in common: they have come to place their faith in Christ. Reading it I was moved not only by the awesome mystery and miracle of conversion, but by the astonishing and endlessly creative means of grace God uses to reach each individual person. In story after story we see a God who loves us, who reaches in, who comes through, and who does not abandon us. Because only a power that is stronger than ourselves can help us overcome ourselves.

—**Rebecca Manley Pippert,** author of *Hope Has Its Reasons* and *Out of the Salt Shaker*

Finding Faith is a fast-moving book about real people in real places with brief narrations that tell of their own discoveries of Jesus Christ. We find out what they felt, what they believe, and the journeys toward God's grace that they have taken.

Sharon Gallagher is a brilliant narrator—always respectful of the people she tells of, yet she enables us to feel the excitement and surprise of the discoveries that they make. I like her spare and low pressure, even understated writing style.

This book helps all who are searching for reality touchstones in their own journeys of faith and doubt. I enthusiastically welcome *Finding Faith* and will not forget the human stories I have read in its pages.

—**Earl F. Palmer,** pastor of University Presbyterian Church in Seattle, author of *The Humor of Jesus* and *The Book That John Wrote*

Sharon Gallagher has opened to us a treasure of new friends and of faith. We enter into their choices, their turnings, their wisdom. This gathering of lives is for the good of our souls, and for the good of our own stories.

—**Kelly Monroe,** editor and coauthor, *Finding God at Harvard: Spiritual Journeys of Christian Thinkers,* founder and director, The Veritas Forum

Radix magazine's distinguished editor, Sharon Gallagher, does, in *Finding Faith,* one of the two things she does better than almost anyone alive: she elicits the voices of the people.

In *Finding Faith* readers are provided a rich smorgasbord of brief histories, vignettes, and testimonies of men and women who came to Jesus Christ after years of neglect or opposition to such faith. Gallagher's subjects are an amazingly diverse crowd. Her introductory comments deftly lace together the narratives without ever minimizing the individuality of her subjects. This is a book about conversion—not the theory but the reality, which is infinitely more interesting. *Finding Faith* would be a great read not just for individuals but for classes and discussion groups. Oh, yes: the second thing Gallagher does better than anyone else is review today's movies, as she does in each issue of *Radix.*

—**David W. Gill,** codirector, Institute for Business, Technology, and Ethics, author of *Becoming Good: Building Moral Character*

Sharon Gallagher focuses in on the transformative experiences of a diverse spectrum of individuals whose encounters with God brought them to Christian faith. A life-affirming, God-affirming book, and a fascinating read!

—**Luci Shaw,** author of *Water My Soul* and *The Angles of Light*

FINDING FAITH

Life-Changing Encounters with Christ

Sharon Gallagher

PageMill Press
A Division of Circulus Publishing Group, Inc.
Berkeley, California

Finding Faith: Life-Changing Encounters with Christ
Copyright © 2001 by Sharon Gallagher
Cover photo by Tom Maday/Photonica
Additional credits on p. 168

Publisher: Tamara Traeder
Editorial Director: Roy M. Carlisle
Art Director: Leyza Yardley
Copyeditor: Jean M. Blomquist
Proofreader: Shirley Coe
Cover Design: Jeff Wincapaw
Interior Design: ID Graphics
Page Composition: A Page Turner/Terragraphics

Typographic Specifications: Body text set in 11.5 Berkeley Book. Heads set in Arial Bold and Arial Black.

Printed in the United States of America.

Library of Congress Cataloging-in-Publication Data
Gallagher, Sharon, 1948–
    Finding faith : life-changing encounters with Christ / Sharon Gallagher.
        p. cm.
    ISBN 1-879290-17-0
    1. Christian converts. 2. Conversion—Christianity. I. Title.

BV4930.G35 2001
248.2'4'0922—dc21

                                                            2001036010

Distributed to the trade by FaithWorks,
a division of National Book Network

10 9 8 7 6 5 4 3 2 1   01 02 03 04 05

To my parents,
Sam and Dorothy Gallagher,
who first taught me the meaning of faith.

I had always felt life first as a story: and if
there is a story there is a storyteller.

—G.K. Chesterton

Contents

VII   DEDICATION

X   PREFACE

XI   ACKNOWLEDGEMENTS

XIII   INTRODUCTION

1   c h a p t e r   o n e   — AMAZING GRACE
How Sweet the Sound, *John Newton* 2 ■ Like a Diamond,
Mary Phillips 5 ■ A Prayer for Help, *Brooks Alexander* 8
■ Born Again, *Charles Colson* 11

15   c h a p t e r   t w o   — A MATTER OF LIFE AND DEATH
The Land of the Living, *Ginny Dost* 16 ■ Art Redeemed,
Elizabeth Claman 19 ■ A Burning Ring of Fire, *Johnny Cash* 22
■ Feeling Brand New, *Maria Muldaur* 24

29   c h a p t e r   t h r e e   — A CHILD SHALL LEAD THEM
A Sunrise Experience, *Fred Vann* 30 ■ A Deeper Motivation,
John Perkins 32 ■ An Abundant Life, *Dorothy Day* 35

38   c h a p t e r   f o u r   — THE LIVING WORD
History with a Design, *Arnie Bernstein* 40 ■ The World's
Story, *Elinor Abbott* 42 ■ Search with All Your Heart, *Joe
Magnusson* 45 ■ Reading the Handbook, *Noel Paul Stookey* 47

51   c h a p t e r   f i v e   — DRAWN TO COMMUNITY
The Displaced Person, *Marian Konrad* 52 ■ Hearing the
Word, *Kathleen Norris* 55 ■ The God Who Cares, *Stephen
Milozski* 58 ■ A New Family, *Heather Weidemann* 62

67   c h a p t e r   s i x   — WHO DO YOU SAY I AM?
I Can't Even Say His Name, *Beverly Liberman* 68 ■ An Academic
Understanding, *Maria Wright* 72 ■ None but Jesus Heard Me,
Sojourner Truth 75 ■ No Other Hope, *Malcolm Muggeridge* 78

83 c h a p t e r s e v e n — BEARING WITNESS
A New Lens, *Mary Stewart Van Leeuwen* 85 ■ Witness of the
Word, *William Everson* 87 ■ Taking the Water, *Treena Kerr* 89
■ A Miracle, *Graham Kerr* 93

97 c h a p t e r e i g h t — BROKEN RELATIONSHIPS
Ultimate Reality, *Phillip E. Johnson* 98 ■ A Cult of One,
Peggy Vanek-Titus 101 ■ A Softer Heart, *Diane Smith* 103

107 c h a p t e r n i n e — THE HOUND OF HEAVEN
The Possibility of Spiritual Adventure, *Dorothy Day* 109
He Was Talking to Me, *Roger Hughes* 111 ■ Jesus Would
Not Leave, *Anne Lamott* 114 ■ The Most Reluctant Convert
in England, *C.S. Lewis* 117

121 c h a p t e r t e n — SIGNS AND WONDERS
The Presence of Love, *Simone Weil* 122 ■ Hearing God's
Voice, *Saint Augustine* 123 ■ A Vision, *Mark Simon* 125
A Dream, *Mary Poplin* 127 ■ The Panther, *Amy Sullivan* 130

133 c h a p t e r e l e v e n — THE CHARACTER OF GOD
The Prodigal, *Marian Dan* 135 ■ Our Great Advocate, *Adam
Huston* 136 ■ The Beginning of Eternal Life, *Thomas Merton* 139
■ A Reflection of God's Beauty, *Krystyna Sanderson* 140

145 c h a p t e r t w e l v e — OTHER VOICES
The Prince of Peace, *Alex Mukulu* 147 ■ More Than a Religion,
Xiao Li Wong 148 ■ A New Program, *Kumar Subramanian* 150
■ The Gift of Salvation, *Pandita Ramabai* 152 ■ The Tao Became
Flesh, *Thomas In-Sing Leung* 156

160 EPILOGUE

162 NOTES

165 BIBLIOGRAPHY

167 ORGANIZATIONS

168 CREDITS

169 ABOUT THE AUTHOR

170 ABOUT THE PRESS

Preface

For many years I've been editing a magazine called *Radix,* "Where Christian Faith Meets Contemporary Culture." Over the years I've interviewed a number of interesting people for the magazine, some famous, some not. Many of those interviews and other *Radix* articles contain conversion stories. This is one of the reasons that publisher Roy Carlisle thought of me when he first had the idea for *Finding Faith.* He knew that I was used to doing interviews and that, in fact, I had already done many that would work well in this book. In its Jesus Movement years, *Radix* was called *Right On,* so some of the earliest pieces in the book are credited to *Right On.*

I did many new interviews for the book and one of the personal plusses was meeting new people and hearing their stories. But it was also a privilege to hear, often for the first time, the faith journeys of friends I've known for years. In addition, I've included some significant conversion stories of earlier heroes of the faith.

Because I live in Berkeley, an academic community, several interviews are with scholars who are friends or friends of friends. Their quests had less to do with intellectual issues than I'd expected. Even though they (and others in this book) had questions answered along the way, getting those questions answered never seemed to be the fundamental issue. In the end, conversion seems to come down to a matter of the heart. As Pascal wrote, "The heart has its reasons which reason does not know."

Acknowledgments

First of all, a warm thank-you to all the people who shared their stories in *Finding Faith*. Their willingness to bare their souls made this book possible.

A special thanks to Roy M. Carlisle, my editor at PageMill Press, who had the initial vision for this book. A lunchtime conversation with the Rev. Mark Labberton of First Presbyterian Church, Berkeley, inspired Roy, who then approached me about the project.

I'm grateful to those friends who helped with suggestions, phone numbers, and e-mail addresses of people with interesting conversion stories. Special thanks to Walt and Ginny Hearn, Bonnie Johnston, and Susan Phillips, as well as Earl Palmer, Dan Curran, David Fetcho, and my parents. Liz Smyth kindly helped with some of the tape transcriptions.

For many years my friends David Gill, Laurel Gasque, Mark Lau Branson, and Jim Wallis have encouraged me to write a book. So to them, thank you—I was listening.

Most of all, I want to thank my husband, Woody, for his support. An excellent writer, he was a sounding board, an editor, and an enthusiastic reader whose encouragement was invaluable.

Introduction

Modern America is a self-proclaimed post-Christian society where, as the media generally portrays it, we live our lives as though God is not part of the picture. People in movies, TV shows, and magazines apparently solve their daily problems and answer their big questions in a world closed off from its Creator.

That may be a true picture of the lives of many Americans, but not of all of them. According to the pollsters, two out of five Americans attend church or synagogue weekly, and even more say they "believe in a personal God."

This book will focus on those who have moved in and out of the pollsters' categories of belief and unbelief, church attendance and nonattendance. In their late teens or early twenties, people often move away from the religious traditions they grew up in. But at a later time in their lives, these same people may once again feel the need for faith and a spiritual home.

Some may be looking for a community, a sense of belonging. Faith might be part of the heritage they want to leave to their children. People entering middle age often find that financial success hasn't brought them the fulfillment they expected. Or they may feel that a deep part of themselves, a spiritual side, has barely been tapped. Some people may be looking for purpose, wanting to know if there is any meaning in life. Others may be curious about the figure at the center of the Christian faith—Jesus Christ. They may be seeking to fill a sense of inner emptiness. The longings of all these people may lead to what we call a "conversion experience."

Varied Paths

The people whose stories follow came from many walks of life—from suburban nominal Christians, to drug addicts and alcoholics, from people who had never thought much about faith, to those who had already been down many alternate paths. For some people, conversion was a gradual process; for others it was a dramatic turnaround that amazed them and those who knew them.

Mary Phillips, for example, deliberately set out to find out whether there was a God who could set her free from drug addiction. But Anne Lamott, whose life was also in crisis, was not entirely pleased when Jesus literally appeared in her life. Some people experienced a spiritual longing throughout their lives but didn't know how to connect with God. Others, like Roger Hughes and Arnie Bernstein, were vehemently anti-Christian when they were younger, but came to reexamine their objections later in life.

What Is Conversion?

The *New International Dictionary of the Church* defines conversion as "a radical change, a transformation, a turning around . . . 'repentance' (turning from) and 'faith' (turning to) are usually seen as the two sides of conversion." The famous image Jesus uses of being "born again" emphasizes how dramatic the event is. To be reborn, you choose to die to your old life. Only then are you given a new one.

The poet Kathleen Norris writes that "'conversion' is a word that at its root connotes not a change of essence but of perspective, a turning round; turning back to or returning; turning one's attention to."[1] One of the root meanings of the word "religion" is to "reconnect" or "retie." Religion is the way people try to reconnect with God. Christians believe that God has provided Jesus Christ as the way for us to make the connection.

So many people mentioned C. S. Lewis as a major influence that it seems appropriate to quote from his book *Mere Christianity*. Responding to people who say that Jesus was a great moral teacher but not the Son of God, Lewis wrote:

> A man who was merely a man and said the sort of things Jesus said would not be a great moral teacher. He would either be a lunatic—on the level with the man who says he is a poached egg—or else he would be the Devil of Hell. You must make your choice. Either this man was and is the Son of God: or else a madman or something worse . . . But let us not come with any patronizing nonsense about His being a great human teacher. He has not left that open to us. He did not intend to.[2]

At some point, we need to decide if Jesus Christ is who He said He is. But conversion involves more than intellectual assent to the deity of Jesus. The book of James tells us that even demons believe that Jesus is the Son of God, but that doesn't mean that they're redeemed. What God wants is obedience, and that begins with an initial act of repentance.

Here we'll talk about conversion as the period of time— long or short—when a man or woman consciously decides to become a Christian, but that decision is just the beginning of the story. Becoming alive to God is a lifelong process with many cycles of repentance and renewal along the way. Frederick Buechner says: "To repent is to come to your senses. It is not so much something you do as something that happens.

True repentance spends less time looking at the past and saying, 'I'm sorry' than to the future and saying 'Wow.'"[3]

What Conversion Is Not

Up until the third century, Christians were a small, persecuted sect. One of many competing religions in the Roman Empire, Christianity was seen as subversive because its members would not worship the emperor as a god. But then the emperor, Constantine, received a vision of a cross in the sky and underwent a dramatic conversion. After becoming a Christian, Constantine declared his whole empire Christian. Over the centuries, this state-decreed conversion has caused confusion about people who are "cultural" Christians (born in "Christian" countries) and people who have actually chosen to follow Christ. At times, militant branches of the church abandoned Jesus' ethic of love and forced their dogma on those they disagreed with.

There were times in European history when Jewish people were persecuted if they didn't convert to Christianity. During the Inquisition, Catholics tortured Protestants to get them to recant, and during the potato famine in Ireland, starving Irish Catholics were told that they would be given food if they converted to Protestantism. But these kinds of "conversions" are not what we're talking about here. They have to do with power, politics, money, and prejudice, but nothing to do with the way God calls people to himself. The Biblical notion of conversion is always based on a free-will decision.

A Few Words about Language

When talking about their conversion experiences, people generally referred to God as "he." In English there is no gender-neutral personal pronoun, and the important truth is that God is personal and relational. W. H. Auden describes the moment Jesus was born in the Bethlehem stable as the time when, "Everything became a you and nothing was an it." Above all, we can't make God an "it."[4]

But referring to God as "he" doesn't mean that God is actually a bearded old man sitting in the clouds. Genesis tells us that "God created humankind in his image, in the image of God he created them; male and female he created them" (Gen. 2:27). God is not a man—both male and female reflect the image of God. Romanian pastor Richard Wurmbrandt said that when he looked into a mirror with his wife at his side, he felt he was seeing a fuller image of God than his own image could reflect.

Jesus taught us to pray to God as our Father in heaven, helping us understand that God loves us as a good parent would. There are many other male metaphors for God throughout the Bible, but there are also female ones. For example, in Isaiah 66:13, God says, "As a mother comforts her child, so will I comfort you." In the New Testament several days before his betrayal and death, Jesus addresses Jerusalem: "How often have I desired to gather your children together as a hen gathers her brood under her wings, and you were not willing!"(Luke 13:34).

Male and female metaphors for God help us to understand God's nature, but they are just metaphors. Old Testament scholar John Otwell has written: "It seems likely that the ancient Israelites believed passionately that their

God, the creator of all that was, transcended gender. Sexuality was a part of God's creation. Therefore it was intrinsically good. Nonetheless, it was part of the creation, not of the Creator who transcended the creation."[5]

In contrast to their pagan neighbors, the Israelites were forbidden to make images, or idols, to represent God, as a human or in any other form. The Israelites even avoided saying his name. The Hebrew name for God was Yahweh— a form of the verb "to be."

Denominations

As you read this book, you may notice that while one person may describe a tradition as being unhelpful to his or her spiritual life, someone else may have come to faith in that same tradition. One explanation is that even within the same denomination, pastors, congregations, and orientations vary widely. Within the same denomination there may be churches that are spiritually alive and those that are not.

Each person comes to God with different needs. For some people worship comes most naturally in a church with stained-glass windows, a pipe organ, and a choir. Others may feel that God has called them to a small, inner-city house church, where they worship with people in an intentional community. This book is not a theological treatise, nor is it making a case for any particular tradition. Each person has related his or her own story without conforming to any specific denominational doctrine. In writing this book I wanted to learn more about how God is working in people's lives. Personally, I've been shaped by a variety of Christian traditions and welcome all truth where it can be found.

An Agenda

But this book does have an agenda—it is specifically about Christian faith. It relates the stories of men and women who, in a variety of ways, both expected and unexpected, have come to faith and are willing to talk about their doubts and fears, their joys and hopes. It is offered to those who want to listen in on how God continues to work in the lives of people today.

CHAPTER ONE

Amazing Grace

I once was lost but now am found;
was blind but now I see.

—John Newton

Grace is a good starting point for a book about conversion. Grace means that God offers us love and redemption despite the mistakes we may have made in our lives. Grace also means that God's love is given freely: it's not something we earn through our own efforts.

By God's grace we can be forgiven when we don't deserve to be. But then we are asked to forgive in the same spirit. The Lord's Prayer brings us up short with the phrase: "Forgive us our debts, as we forgive our debtors."

"Forgiveness" is a theme that recurs in different ways in the stories shared here. Some people sought forgiveness from those they had hurt; others were led to forgive those who had hurt them. All asked for and received God's forgiveness.

One of Jesus' most radical and difficult teachings has to do with forgiveness. One of the disciples asked Jesus how many times you had to forgive someone and suggested "Seven?" (When I was a child and first heard this story, seven seemed like an excessive amount. Forgiving someone two times sounded about right—generously giving the person a second chance.) But Jesus answered the disciple, "Seventy times seven."

Philip Yancey calls this "The New Math of Grace" and says: "I believe Jesus gave us these stories about grace in order to call us to step completely outside our tit-for-tat world of ungrace and enter into God's realm of infinite grace."[6]

We all need God's grace. But some people come to see that need more easily than others. Jesus was often criticized by the "good" religious people of his day for associating with sinners—despised people like prostitutes and those who collected taxes for the Roman invaders. Jesus told his critics that he hadn't come to call the righteous, but the sinners to repentance. He also pointed out that many of the "righteous" people who were judging his companions were "whitewashed tombs"—respectable on the outside, but not so great inside.

The people whose stories follow all came to a place where they realized that they needed God's grace—and found it a good place to be.

How Sweet the Sound ■ ■
John Newton ■ ■

The title of this chapter comes from one of the best-loved hymns in the world. It was written by John Newton in gratitude that God would save even "a wretch like me."

Newton was born in England in 1725, the son of a seafaring father. His mother, a devout Christian, died when Newton was seven. He grew up to be a rebellious teenager and a young man who scorned religion. He drank too much, gambled, and was known for his foul mouth. At times Newton was filled with remorse for the kind of life he was living, but found himself unable to change.

Newton became a sailor like his father, and worked in Africa for a period of time, pressed into service by a slave trader. He eventually escaped that man and returned to England.

In 1748 Newton found himself on board a ship called the *Greyhound,* heading from London to Africa. The weather was hot, and the ship was "unfit"—worn and out of repair. Newton's language was so profane that even the hardened captain and crew were afraid that his blasphemy might attract God's wrath. One night after he had gone to bed, Newton was awakened by a violent storm. His cabin quickly filled with

3

water, and soon a cry came from the deck that the ship was going down. The men tried to pump water out of the hold and lashed themselves to the ship so they wouldn't be washed away. Though badly damaged, the ship did not go down.

All the next day, Newton pumped water and steered the ship. When he finally went to bed at midnight, he began reflecting on his life. He later wrote, "Allowing the Scripture premises, there never was nor could be such a sinner as myself; and then I concluded that my sins were too great to be forgiven.

"I began to think of Jesus whom I had so often derided; I recalled the particulars of his life and death: a death for sins not his own, but, as I remembered, for the sake of those who in their distress should put their trust in Him."[7] Newton still had doubts about Christianity but decided that "upon the Gospel scheme there was a peradventure of hope."

Although they survived the storm, the crew was at sea four more weeks in a battered, leaking ship with dwindling supplies. Their sails were in tatters, which made navigating difficult. Finally, when they had eaten their last bit of food and had just about given up, a gentle wind brought them into port in Lough Swilly, Ireland. Two hours later another storm arose that would have completely demolished the *Greyhound*. Newton said, "About this time, I began to know that there is a God who hears and answers prayers."

It is sometimes implied that after Newton's dramatic shipboard conversion he immediately gave up the slave trade. But the truth isn't that clear-cut. Conversion is the beginning of a process, and while the immediate difference may be dramatic it's never complete.

After his near-death experience at sea, Newton was no

longer the profane person he had been. But his faith was a personal, pietistic one that didn't question the assumptions of a society that had grown wealthy from the slave trade. Newton continued to work in that trade, priding himself on treating the slaves with gentleness. He noted that on one journey he didn't lose a single life—evidence of his good treatment. During this period Newton had no Christian friends or opportunities for education in the faith.

Within a few years, though, he grew to recognize the evil of the slave trade and was deeply ashamed of his part in it. He published an antislavery document, "Thoughts Upon the African Slave Trade." In it he wrote, "I hope it will always be a subject of humiliating reflection to me that I was once an active instrument in a business at which my heart now shudders."

It was in that deep spirit of penitence that he wrote the song "Amazing Grace." After ending his career as a ship's captain, Newton became a minister in Olney, England, where people flocked to hear "the slave trader turned preacher." One of the people who was deeply affected by Newton's preaching was a young aristocrat named William Wilberforce. After his conversion, which was influenced by Newton, Wilberforce organized the movement that brought an end to the slave trade in England.

Like a Diamond ■ ■
Mary Phillips

Mary Phillips was a rebellious teenager who was kicked out of several schools. At the age of seventeen, she was sent to the Maryland State Reformatory for stealing. Eventually she moved to San Francisco where she became addicted to speed (methamphetamine). Soon her life revolved around speed, and she'd stay awake for days at a time while her three-year-old daughter fended for herself as best she could.

One night when she was high on speed and acid, Mary left her daughter unattended in a Laundromat. By the time she went back, the child had been taken into protective custody, and was later put in foster care. After losing her daughter, nothing much mattered to Mary. She found her only escape from guilt and sorrow in drugs. She lived in a succession of speed houses, and at one point she stayed in a closet for months, taking drugs constantly.

Eventually she met and married a drug dealer and they moved from one North Beach hotel to another, evicted for dealing and fighting. Her husband became a successful dealer, and the couple moved to a speed lab where they cooked and sold speed. They made a lot of money and began spending it on heroin.

When they got hooked on heroin, life became even more of a living hell. All their money was spent on drugs, and Mary's husband was arrested several times. Twice during this period Mary overdosed, and her husband (a former Eagle Scout) saved her life with mouth-to-mouth resuscitation.

Then the couple and their baby son were evicted and needed a place to stay. Mary's friends Brooks and Debby, who had recently become Christians, invited Mary and her family to stay with them. Mary knew there was something important going on. She decided that while she was staying with these Christians she'd make an attempt to see whether the Gospel was really true. "I wanted to know whether Jesus could really liberate prisoners. Being an addict, I wanted to know whether Jesus could liberate me. I was watching these Christians like a hawk and decided to intensely concentrate. I read the Bible and prayed, and I would walk down to [the University of California] campus and listen to the preachers."

Mary's perspective began to change. "It was just little things at first," she remembers. "One of the preachers talked about how we should be prepared to enter the kingdom— 'Would we be clothed in the garments of righteousness?' And I remember looking down at my red dress and my chipped red fingernails and thinking, 'You know, I don't think I'm going to be looking too good.'

"But then things got more intense. Like someone would come give me a Christian flyer and they would give me this look like, 'You know what this is.' And then I would feel kind of funny. Sometimes, when someone would preach, people would yell at them or even throw things at them. People would call them names. One day someone threw an orange at the preacher and hit the preacher, and when that happened, I felt like it hit me. Jesus was doing things to show that He was with me."

Mary and her husband had been in Berkeley and off drugs for about a month when she prayed to the Lord and said she wanted to be a Christian. The enormous stress she'd been under was relieved immediately after her prayer.

The next day Mary went back to the campus and met two of the preachers. "I told them that I had always been a pretty wild person and that I was a drug addict and that I didn't know how to be anything else than what I was. I said, 'But I do believe that Jesus is the Son of God.' And then one of the preachers said, 'Would you like to be baptized?' And I said, 'Yes.' And he said, 'Well let's go down to the creek,' and I was dunked in the creek by this street preacher and I went home sparkling like a diamond."

After that Mary read everything she could about her new faith. She remembers, "I read the book of Matthew from the Phillips translation. I even picked up a scrap of *Right On* from the ground and read it. I was still a little crazy when I became a Christian, but I was truly reborn. I never shot up any more drugs after that. I never took heroin again, and I never smoked tobacco again."

Reflecting on her past she says, "I had no plans to give up my lifestyle—in fact I saw no way out. I had been caught in a trap and would have died in it. But I went on a mission to find out whether Jesus could liberate me. He did liberate me, and he still is liberating me."

■ ■ A Prayer for Help
■ ■ *Brooks Alexander*

Brooks Alexander, the friend who took Mary and her family in when they were destitute, was raised in a nominally Christian home. His parents went to church even though they bought into a naturalistic "scientistic" worldview and had no personal spiritual practices. The church they went to talked about Jesus as a great moral teacher, but there was no sense that Jesus was anything more.

To Brooks, Christianity seemed like just another social activity, and by the time he was in university he had developed a strong anti-Christian bias. On campus he was known as an atheist, and he enjoyed baiting Christians with intellectual arguments "designed to destroy the faith of anyone naive enough to believe in the unseen." Eventually he decided that being agnostic was more intellectually respectable than atheism.

As a political science major, Brooks was concerned about warfare in the nuclear age, with its threat of global annihilation. He developed a strong ethos of humanistic idealism and planned to join the diplomatic corps. But as he worked on his master's degree in international affairs, he became disillusioned about the possibility of peace in a world where violence, or the threat of it, is the final arbiter.

Feeling that he could do no good on an international level, Brooks then decided to become an attorney in order to help people with interpersonal disputes. When he worked as a law clerk at an Austin firm, however, he became so disappointed with the actual practice of law that he dropped out of law school in his last year.

Brooks worked for a while as a graphic artist in San Diego, but felt that there was no one in the field ahead of him by five or ten years who had a lifestyle he could even remotely identify with. Eventually he moved to San Francisco where he ran into some old friends from Austin who were into drugs. Brooks experimented with several of them, eventually settling on methedrine (speed) as his drug of choice. On speed he was able to do his artwork with a "furious concentration" that he couldn't achieve on his own. Taking speed was a "power trip," but he soon reached the point where he was either "wired" (in a state of compulsive frenetic activity) or "crashing" (flat on his back in exhaustion). So he moved to the country and began to "come down" from all the methedrine he'd been taking. During this time he began to reflect on his life.

After his disillusionment about changing the world or

changing society, personal relationships were really all he had left, and he felt that his most pivotal relationships had been failures. One night, while staring into a fireplace full of ashes, he realized that "as far as the present was concerned, I used people with some facility (and increasing boredom) but was close to no one." Brooks was painfully aware that there was something fundamentally lacking in his life.

He says, "I saw inescapably what my situation really was. I understood that despite all the true things I had discovered, I had never come close to truth. I knew that despite all the movement in my life, not only had I failed to 'arrive,' I wasn't even really on the path. More frightening than anything else, I had gradually discarded the objects of my caring, one by one. I had begun with a concern for many things and large issues; I was left with the vestiges of a very small and self-centered itch of hedonistic ambition, and even that was perceptively slipping away. I understood instinctively that when that was gone, I would have no real reason to go on living for a single day."

Looking back on that time, Brooks feels that God interpreted his situation as a prayer for help. The next day, through a set of circumstances beyond his control, he was removed from the situation he'd been in and found himself in Berkeley with a new group of people. As he watched two of these people, he was struck by the loving way they treated each other. When he asked them about it, they said that what he'd witnessed came from Jesus Christ.

Brooks remembers, "Those Christians were very tolerant of my groundless arrogance, and indulged my intellectual probing in a cheerful and willing spirit. For approximately a week, I hammered out the various conceptual issues to my own eventual satisfaction in a virtually nonstop conversation.

"I emerged at the end of that time recognizing that in fact I had become a Christian in the course of the week without being able to put my finger on the day or the hour. My Christianity seemed less a profession than a rueful admission, but I was joyful at what I had found. In honest truth, I did not 'find' the Lord; I wasn't looking for him, I was looking for a way out. When I had exhausted my own resources, he was able to find me."

Born Again ■ ■
Charles Colson ■ ■

Charles Colson graduated from law school with honors, rose to the rank of captain in the Marine Corps, was named "outstanding young man of Boston," served as an assistant to a U.S. senator, and became a special counsel to the president of the United States. Quite a success story.

Yet at the height of his political power, he was not universally admired. During his four years of service at the White House, Colson was known as Richard Nixon's hatchet man—a man, according to one media commentator, "incapable of humanitarian thoughts."

In 1974 Colson entered a plea of guilty to obstruction of justice based on his participation in the Nixon White House "dirty tricks." He entered Alabama's Maxwell Prison as the first member of the Nixon Administration to be incarcerated for Watergate-related charges. He also entered the prison as a new Christian.

Colson had a friend named Tom Phillips who had been a business acquaintance during the 1960s. Colson hadn't seen him in four years and when they met in the spring of 1973, Phillips was a totally changed person. When Colson asked him what had happened, Phillips shocked him by saying, "I have accepted Jesus Christ and committed my life to him."

Some months later, Phillips told him that he had become a Christian at a Billy Graham crusade. In addition to telling his own story, Phillips read to Colson from a chapter entitled "The Great Sin" (pride), in C. S. Lewis's *Mere Christianity*. Colson recalls: "That was one of the most painful but significant experiences in my life. As Phillips was reading it—and of course Lewis writes so elegantly—I realized that Lewis was describing me. I had never come to grips with myself, with my own ambitions, with what made Chuck Colson what he was. As my friend read those words, it was a searing experience. I felt as if my whole flesh was being burned. When I left Tom's home that night I broke down in tears.

"Afterward, I took the book and went off with my wife to spend a week's vacation on the Maine coast. I read every paragraph, sentence and line of *Mere Christianity*. I outlined it. The pages were falling out. I always carry a yellow pad and pen with me, and I made two columns: 'There is a God,' 'There isn't a God'; and 'Jesus Christ is God,' 'He isn't God.' It was as if I was preparing for a case. And it was through that that I accepted Christ."

When news of Colson's conversion to Christianity leaked to the press in 1973, the *Boston Globe* commented, "If Mr. Colson can repent of his sins, there just has to be hope for everybody." And Colson agrees, which is why he founded Prison Fellowship, a ministry to prisoners and their families.

As a result of his own transformation, Colson believes in

restoration rather than retribution in the criminal justice system. He says, "I was almost forty-two when I accepted Christ. At best, I was a theist. I thought there was a God because it was sort of absurd that there wouldn't be. But having a personal relationship with Christ was at the bottom of my list. I know how radical my own transformation has been, so I can't look at any body and say, 'It can't happen to him.'"

Colson believes that reconciliation among offenders, victims, their families, and communities should be a concern for Christians, and through his efforts, Prison Fellowship has become one of the world's largest volunteer organizations. He hasn't forgotten the promise he made during his own stay in prison that he would "never forget those behind bars."

■   ■   ■

After the communion service at my church we always hold hands and sing "Amazing Grace." One Sunday I caught myself singing "Amazing grace how sweet the sound that saved a wretch like *you*," which showed that I hadn't been listening very closely to the sermon. But it revealed more than that.

It isn't easy to admit, in the words of the spiritual, that "it's me, oh Lord, standing in the need of prayer." But that admission is a necessary step toward wholeness and renewal. In her book, *Resurrection Psychology*, Peggy Alter talks about what happens when we give up our need for control and open up to God's grace. "We find ourselves unique, special, and beloved—three longings of the human heart. They are gifts to us . . . "[8] How sweet the sound.

CHAPTER TWO

A Matter of Life and Death

Even though I walk through the darkest
valley, I fear no evil; for you are with me;
your rod and your staff—they comfort me.

—Psalm 23:4

In contrast with twenty-first century America, where as one person said, "Death is the new obscenity," earlier generations lived with daily reminders of death. Adults had short life expectancies, infant mortality rates were high, and most people lived on the land and slaughtered their own animals, close to nature's cycles. Until very recently, people worshiped in churches surrounded by cemeteries filled with the graves of those who'd gone before them. And the gravestones often bore reminders such as, "As I am so thou shalt be."

During the Middle Ages, in response to the outbreaks of bubonic plague that decimated Europe's population, death was often personified in art. The famous "dance of death" (seen at the end of Ingmar Bergman's movie *The Seventh Seal*) was painted on churches and cloisters. Death was a character in the most famous medieval mystery play, *Everyman*. Artist Hans Holbein even created an entire alphabet of death, with skeletons surrounding the letters.

In Albrecht Dürer's famous engraving, *St. Jerome in His Study*, the fourth-century scholar is pictured working at his desk. The desk faces a large window, and on a ledge in front of the window is a skull. If Jerome looks out at the beauties of the world, he does so with a reminder of how quickly all things pass.

Today most Americans live in a sanitized world where there are few daily reminders of life's brevity. Oddly, all the violence we see on TV and in movies makes death seem even more unreal and life more cheap. Teenagers and children in America are committing unspeakably violent crimes at an age when courts aren't sure whether they even understand what death is.

Most of us live our daily lives as if they will go on forever. Understandably people aren't eager to confront their own mortality or that of a loved one. But there are times when we find ourselves on the brink of eternity, through accidents, illness, or despair. At these times we may confront the biggest issue in life—our relationship to God.

The Land of the Living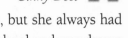
Ginny Dost

Ginny Dost grew up in a troubled home, but she always had a spiritual nature. She went to Catholic school and was drawn to the beauty of the rituals and the sense of the sacred, and for a while she wanted to be a nun.

Her family was poor and Ginny had an intense desire to find out more about the world, so she enlisted in the navy right out of high school and became a nurse. Later she went back to college for a degree in English literature. At that time she started doubting her faith. She still prayed, but she no longer felt connected to God and had stopped going to church.

For a while she practiced Zen meditation and read books by J. Krishnamurti. Ironically it was something Krishnamurti said about "knowing the truth when you see it" that led her to realize that for her Jesus was the truth, but she didn't know how to reconnect. She wasn't sure how to worship or how to believe.

Then she met and fell in love with Tom, and they became engaged. Six weeks before their wedding they were out sailing on San Francisco Bay in Tom's twenty-nine-foot catamaran—

intending to join a race at Point Richmond. Suddenly the wind shifted and the boat started to capsize. Everyone jumped into the water, but as they did, Ginny was caught in the rigging and held beneath the surface.

Tom couldn't see her, and was yelling to their friends, "Ginny's gone. She's gone."

Ginny says, "I was struggling to get loose and was sure I was dying. I prayed, 'Lord, I'm in your hands,' and then I was filled with a great sense of peace. I must have lost consciousness and gone limp, and somehow when I stopped struggling I got loose of the rigging and floated toward the surface. All of a sudden Tom felt something bumping against him, and it was me. I had long hair then, and Tom pulled me up out of the water by my hair. I was unconscious and had turned totally blue."

The next thing Ginny remembers is hearing voices and waking up in an ambulance. Even though she was in critical condition, she told the paramedics to take her to Alta Bates, the hospital where she worked. They should have taken her to a closer hospital, but they took her to Alta Bates—which was a good thing. That afternoon a doctor was on duty whose specialty was drowning victims and treating pulmonary edema. Ginny now feels that it was divine intervention that this specialist was there when she came in.

As Ginny was in the hospital recuperating, coworkers who turned out to be Christians "came out of the woodwork" to visit her and witness to her. She found it all a little overwhelming. One man gave her John Stott's *Basic Christianity,* which helped her understand what Christian faith is all about.

Cully Anderson, the pastor who was to perform Ginny and Tom's marriage ceremony, came to visit her and read to her from Psalm 27—a passage that meant a great deal to her at the time and has helped her through other life crises. Verses 13 and 14 were especially meaningful to her: "This I believe: I shall see the goodness of Yahweh, in the land of the living. Put your hope in Yahweh, be strong, let your heart be bold, put your hope in Yahweh." (JB.)

Ginny gradually underwent a transformation but still wasn't sure how to worship God or reconnect to the church. Her husband, Tom, knew she loved the Inklings, a group of writers that included C. S. Lewis, J. R. R. Tolkien, and Dorothy Sayers. He took her to a Presbyterian church whose pastor, Earl Palmer, quoted these writers liberally in his sermons. Once there, Ginny felt she had found her church home. She had reconnected.

Art Redeemed ■ ■
Elizabeth Claman ■ ■

Elizabeth Claman was raised without any real sense of God or faith. At times she was exposed to Christianity and Judaism, but not in a way that touched her, and she never made any sort of commitment.

Elizabeth graduated from the California Institute of Art with honors and began selling her paintings. She soon found that while she felt energized and alive when she was involved in the act of painting, when she was finished she felt depressed.

Elizabeth had always been attracted to film as an art form, so she moved to Los Angeles to work in the film industry. She began getting production jobs and worked on some interesting projects, including Woody Allen's *Sleeper.* Then she began designing costumes for TV commercials and making a lot of money. But, as she tells it, the lifestyle wasn't rewarding.

"Over the course of the next two years, I got crazier and crazier. The people I worked with were bright and talented and making outrageous salaries by cranking out thirty- and sixty-second pieces of film designed to coerce housewives and children into spending money on things they didn't need."

Elizabeth grew more and more frustrated. She started saving money and dreamed of buying some time and freedom. Eventually she moved to a cabin in the woods where she was able to spend a year producing drawings, paintings, collages, and sculpture, as well as writing fiction and poetry. Elizabeth was finally living her dream, but it didn't make her happy—in fact, she grew more and more depressed. And she began thinking about suicide.

She'd had an early marriage but left when her husband became a Christian. Her daughter from that marriage lived with Elizabeth's ex-husband and his new wife. Elizabeth felt her daughter was happy there and didn't need her. In fact, when Elizabeth examined her life, she felt generally unneeded and useless.

She decided that she would kill herself on New Year's Day after she'd taken her daughter to the airport to fly home to her father. But she felt that she needed his forgiveness first, so she called the house where he lived. Another woman who lived in the house answered the phone and started sharing her love for Jesus. Elizabeth prayed with the woman, who advised her to join a Christian fellowship as soon as possible.

Elizabeth did join a Christian group and began reading the Bible. She remembers, "I was deeply moved by the miraculous work of our Lord. His death on Calvary made me cry with sorrow and shame. His resurrection and its promise made me cry with joy and hope. I was led to see how badly I had behaved in all my relationships—with my mother, ex-husband, daughter, everyone. I had been blind and selfish and cruel. The Lord made my heart ache for so much wrong, and he made it full of love for all those people. He made me turn and ask their forgiveness."

The Christian group that Elizabeth had joined was a legalistic fundamentalist sect whose leaders told her to destroy all her artwork. They were very strict, and she chafed at their rules and demands. She eventually left the group but didn't look for another place to worship because the sect she'd been in had condemned all other churches.

Without fellowship Elizabeth found herself "groveling back at art's altar." She says, "Other artists said I'd finally come into my own. As my ego grew, it got harder to see Jesus. My prayer life faded. My morning devotions got replaced by exploring my rediscovered neuroses in my journal. But I still believed that the sect I had come out of was the true church and felt that I needed to get art out of my system before I could go back."

Then Elizabeth went on a trip through Italy and Greece and spent wonderful times on isolated mountaintops and in ancient churches. Many of the extraordinary works of art she was viewing were dedicated to Christ and his church, and this confused Elizabeth because she'd been taught that no works of art could be pleasing to God—they were vain distractions.

When she returned to San Francisco, Elizabeth felt confused and anxious and far from God. On Christmas Eve of that year she prayed that God would reveal himself in some powerful way, to show that he was still interested in her.

She says, "What happened wasn't quite what I had in mind, but it certainly did work! I ended up in the hospital after hemorrhaging for sixteen hours. The doctors never did figure out what it was, but I knew. Over the next week, as I recovered, I felt like a newborn child: weak, simple, helpless. I lay in bed and read the Bible and praised God."

Elizabeth was eventually led into fellowship with a group of Christians who didn't judge or condemn her but encouraged her to go on from exactly where she was. She also found a network of Christians who supported her need to a write and create art. Now she says, "I've learned that God gives us talents and gifts for good reason and that it's our responsibility to use them in ways that glorify him and show our love for one another."

■ ■ A Burning Ring of Fire
■ ■ *Johnny Cash*

Johnny Cash grew up in a Christian family. In adolescence when his mother first heard his now-famous bass voice, she told him it was a gift from God.

When Cash started writing music and performing, he wanted to sing gospel music but his producer, Sam Phillips, thought that there wasn't enough money in it.

In the late 1950s, while he was touring, Cash took his first amphetamine, and he liked the effect. It made him feel energetic and it banished his shyness. But the longer he took the pills, the more pills it took to get the same rush. The drug binges started taking up more and more of his life, and when he was sober the withdrawal symptoms were ghastly.

After taking thousands of the pills, he felt that the drugs had separated him from his family and from God. His career was suffering also. He started canceling performances, and when he did perform the drugs made his throat dry and affected his voice. When friends warned him that the drugs could kill him, he got angry and told them that he could handle it. But he eventually reached a point where he felt "barely human" and was convinced that he had wasted his life.

One day he decided to end it all. He drove out to a group of caves on the Tennessee River with the intention of getting lost in the deep caverns and never coming back. He crawled farther and farther back into the cave system and finally stopped when the batteries on his flashlight failed. Then he lay down to die.

As he wrote later, "The absolute lack of light was appropriate, for at that moment I was as far from God as I have ever been . . ." Cash thought that God had abandoned him. But he hadn't. Cash "felt something very powerful start to happen to me, a sensation of utter peace, clarity and sobriety. I didn't believe it at first. I couldn't understand it. How, after being awake for so long and driving my body so hard and taking so many pills—dozens of them, scores, even hundreds—could I possibly feel all right?

"The feeling persisted, though, and then my mind started focusing on God."[9]

In Nickajack Cave, Cash became convinced that God was in charge of his life. He knew that he wanted to live, but now wasn't sure whether he could escape the caves. But he managed to slowly crawl out of the cave, where he found his wife and mother looking for him outside. Over the next weeks

Cash went through a very painful period of withdrawal, experiencing horrible nightmares and hallucinations. Through all this he was supported by his family who "formed a circle of faith" around him.

Sobriety remained a struggle for Cash, but, trusting in God, he took it one day at a time. Commenting on his song, "Won't Back Down," Cash said, "I believe in God. And he's been the power, the nucleus, and the very soul of my work. And it's a positive force that will never be denied in my life and in my heart."[10]

■ ■ Feeling Brand New
■ ■ *Maria Muldaur*

Maria Muldaur grew up in New York City as an Italian Catholic. But when she became an adolescent and her love life started picking up, it became harder for her to go to confession.

"I was no longer saying, 'I disobeyed my mother three times.' It got to be a game of going to the priests who had the most lenient confessions. The Irish priests were the toughest; the Italians were more lenient. But if you had a really sordid, juicy confession, you'd go to a Puerto Rican neighborhood where the priest barely understood you anyway."

Maria was also getting involved in the bohemian scene in Greenwich Village and began performing all kinds of roots music: blues, gospel, bluegrass. She played for a while with the Jim Kweskin jug band before going her own way.

She had an enormous hit with her first solo album, *Midnight at the Oasis*. And the success threw her for a loop. She felt unprepared for making all the executive decisions involved in running a very visible career. She was given bad financial advice and spent all her money freely on her friends.

Maria was living in Los Angeles at that time, as a base for her career. But she'd had a daughter, Jenny, during her marriage to musician Geoff Muldaur and decided that the L.A. show-business scene was not a good place to raise her. So she moved to Marin County in Northern California.

Maria hadn't really thought much about her relationship to God for years, but then her daughter was involved in a near-fatal car accident. Maria recalls that difficult time: "I sat outside the operating room where surgeons were putting tiny pieces of my daughter's skull back together, and words from Bob Dylan's newly released *Slow Train Coming* ran through my head audibly and word for word. It was as if I'd memorized them. The line 'When you gonna wake up' came through especially loud and clear. It challenged me to reexamine my priorities.

"I spent those seven hours of surgery, the most traumatic in my life, praying and 'listening' to Dylan's new songs. My daughter was completely healed and within weeks was back to her mischievous self."

Someone gave Maria a Bible, which she began reading. Then about a month later, she accompanied her record producer to a large Pentecostal church in Los Angeles where she went forward during an altar call to receive Christ.

She remembers, "In a back room full of other people who'd also come forward, an old black woman came up and laid hands on me. At that point I began speaking in an unknown language. It felt as if a tube of light was running from my head to my toes and back up out of my vocal cords."

At the time she didn't understand what was happening. But later someone explained to her that she was speaking in a supernatural language given to communicate directly from her heart to God.

"No one ever mentioned the term 'born again' to me at that time, but I walked out of that church feeling brand new. I was looking at the world as if a veil had been lifted from my eyes."

After a few months of being a Christian, Maria began to realize that she didn't need to be on alcohol or drugs to be "loose and groovy." Now she feels that she can perform and it's the real her having fun.

Shortly after her conversion, Maria put together an album of gospel songs with a group of friends. The album was recorded at a small club in Los Angeles. Maria describes how that felt: "It was really great praying together before rehearsal instead of snorting cocaine. So much more got done because we had one focus and purpose, and that was a refreshing change. It was amazing that we could all even fit on that tiny stage. We joked that it was because we all left our egos at home."

Commenting on her life as a Christian musician, she says: "I've always felt that music is one of the special arts; its main purpose is to spread light and joy to people on earth. Maybe the Lord needs to get as many instruments as possible tuned up right now."

■　　　■　　　■

During the time when wars were still largely fought in arm-to-arm combat, there was a saying: "There are no foxhole atheists." Crouching in a muddy trench with bullets flying over their heads, soldiers would turn to God with desperate prayers.

This chapter started out with words from Psalm 23, the most famous psalm written by David, the biblical hero who later became King of Israel. David was no stranger to combat. He had been a musician in the court of King Saul. But when David became a military hero, admired and loved by the people, Saul was jealous and plotted to kill him. Warned of this plot, David and his supporters fled Jerusalem and were chased through the desert by Saul's soldiers. This experience may have inspired another Psalm—"Hear my cry, O God; listen to my prayer. From the end of the earth I call to you, when my heart is faint. Lead me to the rock that is higher than I; for you are my refuge" (Psalm 61; 1 &2).

David often referred to God as his "rock." To a man doing battle in the shifting desert sand, a rock would be a crucial point of reference—the one stable thing. David and his men also found refuge in a cave, a cleft sheltered by rock.

When the sands of life are shifting around us and we are unmoored, confused, or in danger of being overwhelmed, we too can cry out to David's "rock" and have our prayer heard.

CHAPTER THREE

A Child Shall Lead Them

Truth reveals itself to love.

—Leo Tolstoy

In his book *The Spiritual Life of Children,* Robert Coles talks about his early years as a psychologist. He was taught that spirituality was outside the bounds of the therapeutic process. So when he began seeing children as patients and some of them talked to him about their relationship with God, he showed little interest. One little girl in particular talked about her faith at almost every session, and each time she did Coles would change the subject.

One day the little girl confronted the psychologist, asking him how, when he acted as if he cared about her, he could ignore something that was such an important part of her life. That conversation deeply impressed Coles, and from that point on he did address the spiritual lives of his patients.

An adult might have picked up on Cole's cues that this was an unacceptable subject and been silenced. But the little girl, in refusing to ignore an important part of her reality, transformed the career of a Harvard psychologist who was to become an internationally renowned author.

The Gospel of Luke recounts that at the height of his ministry, people brought children to Jesus hoping that he would touch them. "When the disciples saw it, they sternly ordered them not to do it. But Jesus called for them and said, 'Let the little children come to me, and do not stop them; for it is to such as these that the kingdom of God belongs. Truly I tell you, whoever does not receive the kingdom of God as a little child will never enter it'" (Luke 18:15-17).

Children don't have the layers of cynicism that adults have developed for self-protection in a rough world—they are more trusting. As adults we have to rediscover that childlike spirit and come to God in openness, faith, and hope. We can all learn a lot about God's kingdom by watching children, and some people are led to faith by their own children.

A Sunrise Experience ■ ■
Fred Vann ■ ■

Fred Vann, an engineer and businessman, says that even though he had no church background, when he turned thirty, around the time of the birth of his second daughter, he decided that it was time for the family to join a church. He says, "I didn't know where the idea came from: nobody told me to do this. But now I believe it was inspired by the Holy Spirit."

When the family moved to Walnut Creek, California, they joined the Walnut Creek Presbyterian Church because they had a good Sunday school. Fred says, "I was a nominal Christian at the time. One of the things most indicative of that was that I drove my kids to Sunday school, and then I'd drop them off and go home and work in the yard. We'd joined the church, but Christianity didn't influence our lives very much. My wife and I became active in the church, but I was a nominal Christian until my late forties."

When Fred's daughters were teenagers, they were very active in Young Life, a Christian ministry to high school students. "When my second daughter, Leslie, became a born-again Christian, she got my wife and me involved in Bible Study Fellowship and that changed my life. At some point during the years when I was in the Bible study, I was introduced to the writings of C. S. Lewis, and his book *Mere Christianity* really hit home with me. I loved the way Lewis wrote and thought. And then, because of my daughter's interest, I got involved in Young Life as well."

When some Young Life leaders invited Fred on a trip to the East Coast to check out several inner-city ministries, he agreed to join them. For one week, Fred went to a camp outside Philadelphia and stayed in a cabin with inner-city youths—the only adult and the only white guy. "At one point we were told to go out, into nature, and take an hour to think about what Jesus meant in our lives. So on this moonlit night with snow on the ground, I went out and leaned against a tree looking down at a little creek.

"That night I really communicated with God and made sure that I was committed to Jesus Christ. But there were four things that over time changed me from being a nominal Christian to becoming a born-again Christian: being in a Bible study, the books of C. S. Lewis, the influence of Young Life and my pastor, Bill Stoddard."

For some people conversion can be pinpointed to a particular dramatic event, but for others it is a long process. Fred says, "When I lived in Mendocino, my habit was to sit down at my desk before dawn to read and study. When I sat down it would be dark outside; then at some point I'd look up out over the ocean and it would be light outside. When did it change from dark to light? It was a gradual thing, and that's the way my conversion was. But it was prompted by loving my daughters so much and seeing the kind of commitment they made to Jesus Christ."

■ ■ A Deeper Motivation
■ ■ *John Perkins*

As a black man growing up in rural Mississippi, John Perkins experienced the cruelty of poverty and racism. His mother died when he was young, and he and his siblings were raised by their grandmother, with the five children sleeping in a corncrib for a bed.

As a twelve-year-old boy, John once worked all day as a farm laborer for a white man, expecting the going rate of $1.50 for a day's labor. At the end of the day, the man gave John fifteen cents. And though he was insulted, he couldn't show it; he had to pocket the fifteen cents and walk away. But from then on, he analyzed everything from an economic perspective and was determined not to remain a victim.

Another crucial experience for John was when his beloved older brother, a World War II hero, was killed by white people six months after he returned from the war. John thought of Southern white churches as being complicit in this kind of violence, with pastors who didn't speak out about racism or who were racists themselves. He had been to some black churches and viewed the people who went to them as victims whose religion was keeping them submissive to an oppressive structure.

John felt that as a black person in Mississippi he had two options: he could accept the existing system and become dehumanized, or he could resist the system and end up in jail or killed, like his brother. As an adult, he decided to move to California, hoping to get ahead economically. He eventually got a good-paying job, but he noticed that the successful people were usually not very religious. He felt that the Christians he met were the kind of people who would never really make it in the world.

But then John's son started attending Good News Clubs and Child Evangelism classes. "My son would come home and say verses before we ate our meals. I could see that something beautiful was developing in him that I knew nothing about. I had no experience of seeing Christianity in a personal life that was beautiful and good. He would always ask me to go with him to church, and so, finally, because I enjoyed his company so much, I decided to go."

John began going to his son's church and became intrigued by a series the pastor was doing on the teaching and the life of the apostle Paul. When John heard what Paul had endured for his faith, he wondered why anyone would risk so much for religion. John had been operating his life based on economic incentives, but he recognized that the apostle had a deeper motivation. So he began to study the Bible on his own at home.

"Then one night the Holy Spirit was able to take the word of God and apply it to my own life. I found out that I could give my life to Jesus Christ, and he would take care of my sin. I didn't have any solutions for what I'd been struggling with in my life, but for the first time I had an inward peace."

John's conversion eventually led him back to Mississippi, where he founded Voice of Calvary, a ministry that helps people with health care, job training, food, and clothing. As a community where black and white Christians live together, Voice of Calvary also provides an ongoing witness against racism, for the sake of both black people and white people.

John recalls his experience one night when he and twenty-two other black people were almost beaten to death in a Mississippi jail: "That night when those men were beating us, I realized for the first time what racism was doing to white people. I looked at those people and felt sorry for them. They had on their badges, and they had all this need to hurt people in order to feel a sense of worth. That's what racism does to people, and the church isn't confronting that. But I believe that the gospel, the love of Jesus Christ, is stronger than the Southern tradition."

An Abundant Life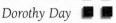
Dorothy Day

Dorothy Day, the founder of the Catholic Worker Movement, is known to many of us as a small gray-haired saint who spent her life working on behalf of the poor and disenfranchised. But Dorothy didn't come to faith easily. Although she'd been drawn to Christianity from an early age, she fought her attraction to God.

As a young woman, Dorothy went to Washington, D.C., to join a group of suffragettes who were picketing the White House. The women were jailed and put in a cold, dark prison where they went on a hunger strike. Feeling completely miserable, Dorothy asked for a Bible. On the fourth day of her hunger strike, a Bible was finally bought to her and she read it eagerly.

She was grateful for the comfort she found in the Psalms, but she still resisted God.

When she left prison, Day viewed her prison-cell need for God as a weakness that she was ashamed of. So she put religion out of her mind and resumed her life in the world, under the influence of friends who discouraged her interest in God.

During this time of her life, Day worked as a journalist in New York City, spending her free time in bars discussing politics with radical friends, including the playwright Eugene O'Neill. Sexual freedom was part of the group's credo, and Dorothy experienced several heartbreaking love affairs. Though her social life and her work kept her busy, something was missing. During that period, she lived near St. Joseph's Church on Sixth Avenue. Day was fascinated by the people she watched going into the church. She longed for the faith and beauty that these people had in their lives.

She eventually fell in love with a man named Forster Batterham, who was a biologist and an anarchist. They moved to a fisherman's cottage on Staten Island where Dorothy worked as a freelance writer and enjoyed living in the small beachside community. Forster was an outdoorsman who introduced Dorothy to a new appreciation of the natural world, which led Dorothy to a love for the Creator. But it was the birth of her daughter, Tamar, that dramatically changed Dorothy's life.

Writing about this time, Day says: "The final object of this love and gratitude was God. No human creature could receive or contain so vast a flood of love and joy as I often felt after the birth of my child. With this came the need to worship, to adore."[11]

Dorothy was befriended by a nun in the fishing village who, with whatever was at hand, made daily soup for a straggly group of the island's needy. Dorothy was immediately drawn to the nun and her practices and was slowly won over to a Christian faith that satisfied both her need to worship and her need to serve the poor.

This Christian commitment was met with hostility by her radical friends, including her baby's father, who saw it as a defection to the establishment. Becoming a Christian and having a child also made Dorothy want to normalize the relationship with Forster, which led to more tension. To Forster, marriage would be a betrayal of his free-love ethic.

Although she had wanted to create a real marriage with Forster, after their split, Dorothy was never to have a traditional family life. Instead, in a slum neighborhood of New York City, she created an extended family, a community of like-minded Christians who joined her to run a soup kitchen, a homeless shelter, and *The Catholic Worker* newspaper. Over the years, her work has inspired others to start Catholic Worker houses all across the country.

A recent movie about Day's life showed how difficult living with the destitute can be—the bad smells, the drunkenness, the mental illness, and the abuse. Day continued in this work her entire life, choosing to love the unlovable, showing the homeless and needy God's love, the love she opened herself up to at the birth of her child.

■   ■   ■

Through loving their own children, the people in this chapter were drawn to an understanding of God's great love for them—his desire to be in a relationship with them as his children. John Perkins and Fred Vann opened their hearts to God through the example of their children's faith—the gift of faith often comes more naturally for children.

When Sam, the son of my pastor Mark Labberton, was two years old, he engaged his father in an interesting theological conversation. While Mark was giving him his bath, Sam said that God had been talking to him. Mark asked what God had said, and Sam answered, "God said, 'Yes'!"

We may need the ears of a child to help us hear God saying "Yes."

CHAPTER FOUR

The Living Word

*Scripture has the ability to break apart
every deathly, cyclical activity
we have the power to devise,
and to make us whole again . . ."*

—Larry Woiwode

On an episode of the TV police show *NYPD Blue,* the young police officer, Danny, is overcome with personal problems that he can't handle. He asks Diane, an older officer, "How do I live my life?" Diane, who feels she doesn't have any answers, says, "And me without my manual."

Christians do have a manual; we've been given the Bible to help guide us through life. But the Bible isn't a manual in the sense of just being a book of rules. It contains rules, like the Ten Commandments; spiritual guidelines, like the Beatitudes; and the two great commandments that Jesus gave his disciples: Love God with all your heart, and love your neighbor as you love yourself.

But the Bible also relates the stories of people, both holy and unholy, who have struggled with God. Most importantly, it tells us about the life of Christ.

And there is more to the Bible than the sum of its parts. Jacques Ellul has written: "Only the word conveys the truth of a religious message. What the written word needs is not to be considered the source of a mere code, law, or formula, or of an indefinitely repeated prayer. It must be taken as its source and given rebirth, not by repetition, but by an inspiration that reopens it."[12]

Personally I've often opened the Bible to some familiar passage to find that it speaks to me in a new way, addressing my life circumstances that day, with surprising insight and immediacy.

People that I interviewed repeatedly related encounters with the Bible as a "living" book. Those who intended to read it as an important piece of world literature found themselves gripped in ways they'd never expected. Some people had their lives changed by reading a single verse.

Dan O'Grady found this out. One night after he'd had a very bad fight with his wife, Dan was so frustrated and angry that he left his house. He started walking and found himself passing the church that he'd been attending. As he walked through the parking lot some people called out to him, "Hi, Dan. Did you come for the Bible study?"

Dan was completely surprised by this and mumbled a reply, but he did join the people inside the church. It turned out to be a group of charismatic Catholics who'd invited Dan to his first Bible study.

Intrigued by what he was reading with the group, Dan also started reading the Gospel of John at home. He opened the Bible and read: "I am the way, the truth, and the life. No one comes to the father except through me" (John 14:6). As he read these words, he realized for the first time who Jesus really was.

Dan says: "I found God's word to be sharp. It really cuts through the bone and marrow. Through this experience I began a new relationship with Christ, which over time has completely changed my life." For Dan and others in this chapter, reading the Bible led to conversion. Many other people found that they felt an overwhelming desire to read Scripture immediately *following* their conversion.

History with a Design ■ ■
Arnie Bernstein ■ ■

Arnie Bernstein's father was born within the walls of the Old City of Jerusalem where he was raised to be an Orthodox rabbi. But in reaction to the Nazi holocaust, he became an atheist and eventually moved to New York City.

Despite his loss of faith, Arnie's father was keenly interested in Jewish culture and was an ardent Zionist. Arnie's parents encouraged him in intellectual and artistic pursuits, and he became a champion chess player. But this success did not bring him happiness. He began to feel that chess was irrelevant and to question whether life had any meaning. Arnie began to see life as a giant chess game, where people were pawns in the hands of politicians, financiers, and religious leaders. "I wasn't even sure whether I was on the right side, or which side was winning, or even if there were two sides."

His mind sought design but all he could see was confusion, in his life and in the world. He began studying history hoping that it would supply him with the order and answers he sought. But Arnie concluded that the only thing history teaches is that humanity has learned nothing from history.

Then he began reading the story of the Jewish people, "a history written in blood." Arnie traced the persecution of the Jewish people through the centuries, which culminated in the "enlightened" twentieth century with the Nazi holocaust that annihilated six million Jews.

As a result of his studies, Arnie says: "I became very hostile toward 'Christians' at whose hand most of the suffering was dealt. . . . I came to conclude that 'Christians' were my worst enemies and that Jesus Christ must have been the worst anti-Semite who ever lived. I became extremely bitter—not only bitter at the world, which I saw represented in Hitler, but also at myself—for I was not able to find any answers to my own questions about the purpose of life. Everyone became my enemy. I saw a potential Nazi in everyone about me, including my closest friends. I felt that I could trust no one, not even myself."

Then one day Arnie began seriously studying the Bible. As he studied it he was struck by how close its description of corrupt humanity matched the conclusions he'd come to. The more Arnie read the Bible, the more he agreed with its description of the world. He found that the Bible talked about a design in history, with God as the master designer. He was also impressed with what it said about the past, present, and future course of Jewish history.

Arnie found that the Jesus Christ described in the Bible was very different from the stereotype he was familiar with: "Far from being a white, middle-class, Gentile, Nordic war god born in Kansas City, I found that he was a Jew, probably dark by Western standards, poor, a 'conscientious objector,' born in a ghetto in the Middle East, and a defender of truth and justice."

Over time Arnie made a clear distinction between the crimes of Christendom and the person of Jesus Christ. As he continued to study the Bible, Arnie became convinced that Jesus Christ was the promised Messiah of the Old Testament, that he had been crucified and risen from the dead.

But though he was intellectually convinced, Arnie hadn't experienced a spiritual encounter with God: "One evening I asked God to make real to me these truths, to come into my life, and give me the power to live now, and forever. I pleaded 'God, in the name of the Messiah Jesus Christ, come into my life.' Since that time God has given Arnie the purpose in life that he sought. He went on to study theology and is now an archpriest in the Antiochian Orthodox Church.

■ ■ The World's Story
■ ■ *Elinor Abbot*

Elinor Abbot was raised on a small family farm in New Hampshire. Although her family attended a Congregational church, she doesn't remember any talk about knowing Jesus personally—but some seeds were sown. Elinor remembers that the pastor's wife came back from a trip to Israel talking enthusiastically about seeing places where Jesus had walked. For the first time Elinor thought, "Hey, maybe this guy really lived."

Elinor was a rebellious teenager. After high school, she was expelled from a couple of colleges and became more and more wild. As she entered her twenties, she felt contempt for religion and religious things. She ended up going to an art school in Boston during the sixties and says, "All that was going on in the sixties was part of my life then."

After art school, Elinor wanted to study the relationship between art and society. She ended up at Brandeis University working for a Ph.D. in anthropology. She eventually decided to do a dissertation on kinship and marriage in colonial Massachusetts. As part of that study, she wanted to research her own family history in its early New England context.

While doing this research, Elinor realized that she didn't know the Bible well enough to understand much of what was going on in seventeenth-century New England. She read that Cotton Mather, the famous Puritan preacher, read the Bible six times a year. And she thought, "I haven't even read the Bible through once. As an educated person I should really read it."

So she got her old Sunday School presentation Bible out and saw that her childhood minister had written a verse on the front page. The verse was: "Hear, O Israel: the Lord is our God, the Lord alone" (Deuteronomy 6:4). As Elinor read the Bible, she continued working on her Ph.D. at Brandeis, which had been founded by the American Jewish community but was open to anyone. As she read the Old Testament, current events in the Middle East, like the Six Days War, echoed her reading.

"As I went through the Old Testament, I could see what was coming. I understood that the way was being prepared for Jesus to walk onto the stage as the promised Messiah. I was beginning to be convinced that this was really the world's story.

"But I didn't really give up and come out of the woods with my hands up until somewhere between John and Acts. At the end of John's gospel, I was very moved by the story of Thomas and his honest doubts. Thomas stands for all of us in a way. Jesus says, 'Blessed are you, Thomas, for believing.' And then it's like Jesus looks right out of the pages of the Bible and says to us, 'And blessed are those who have not seen and believe.' I was eventually and reluctantly persuaded that all that I was reading was true."

Meanwhile, people on Elinor's dissertation committee were becoming alarmed. One of them told her, "You know this will really ruin your career in anthropology. There just aren't any Christian anthropologists."

But Elinor was experiencing "that irresistible grace that Calvin talked about," and there was no way that she could abandon her new faith for the sake of her career.

She began teaching at the University of New Hampshire at the same time that she was writing her dissertation. She got involved with InterVarsity, a Christian group on campus, and a Christian faculty member gave her information about Wycliffe, an organization that sends people around the world to translate the Bible.

When Elinor contacted Wycliffe, they said, "We've been praying because we need anthropologists and helicopter pilots." She said, "Well, I can't do much about the helicopters, but I am an anthropologist."

Elinor joined Wycliffe and began learning how anthropology and missions could actually work together. For years, she worked with Mayan people in southern Mexico until the area was closed because of guerrilla activity. She now teaches at a Wycliffe training center in Dallas, Texas, and works as an international anthropology consultant for translating teams around the world.

■ ■ Search with All Your Heart
■ ■ *Joe Magnusson*

Another important part of Elinor's story was the influence that her sister and her sister's husband, Joe, had on her life. Joe was a Marine during the Second World War and had gone into Japan as part of the occupation force after the atomic bombs had been dropped. He actually lived in a bombed-out factory off the shore of the Nagasaki harbor.

After he returned home, he married and worked as an engineer. But Joe was struggling with questions. "Who am I? Why am I here? What is it all about? What are we going to do for our kids?" So he and his wife started searching. They checked out churches near their home and finally joined one.

Joe recalls: "I went to the pastor with all my questions about the meaning of life and he said, 'Read the Bible and you'll find your answers there.' I came across a verse that really became my conversion verse, Jeremiah 29:13. 'You'll find me when you search for me with all your heart.'

"It was a message given by God to Israel before their captivity in Babylon; however, the promise was held out and I took it for myself."

For many years Joe and his wife tried to talk to Elinor about Christian things, but she just laughed at them. When she was studying anthropology, Joe and his wife went to the World's Fair in New York where they saw some materials from the Wycliffe Bible translators. They thought the material might interest Eleanor because it was about native peoples. But when they gave Elinor this literature, she was even more outraged at "all this missionary stuff." She recalls being very rude when they gave it to her. She also remembers that Joe was always long-suffering and did not take offense.

One of the things that she had counted against her sister and brother-in-law was that, from her perspective, they had always gone to their "safe little white churches" and were unable to deal with people in trouble. To Elinor it seemed like the kind of Christianity that pulled its skirts up around itself to avoid getting dirty with problem people. Elinor thought she was better than that because she and her friends were interested in helping the kind of people that Christians weren't interested in.

But God was at work with Joe and his wife. They sold their house and bought a storefront building in Hyannisport. They turned the whole thing into a drop-in center for runaway kids and street people and ran the center for a number of years. They helped many people and, without knowing it, undermined one of Elinor's defenses against Christianity.

■ ■ Reading the Handbook
■ ■ *Noel Paul Stookey*

Noel Paul Stookey had already achieved enormous success as a singer/songwriter with Peter, Paul, and Mary when he began his quest to find some kind of meaning in life. He had been listening to a lot of Bob Dylan lyrics and arranged to meet Dylan at Woodstock. He wanted information and knew Dylan well enough to say he'd like to meet with him. Dylan agreed and when they met, Stookey asked him, "Well, all this new stuff's happening, Bob. Where do you think it's at?" Dylan answered, "Well, I don't know; where do you think it's at?" Stookey remembers the rest of the conversation:

I replied, "Well, blah blah blah Maharishi, and blah blah blah Eastern mysticism, and blah blah blah the Beatles." Then I said, "Whereas your songs in the past have always related to what's happening, I don't see you addressing yourself to spiritual values. It's one thing to point your finger, and it's another thing to be of encouragement, you know. So where is your music taking you now?" Dylan answered, "Well, wait till you hear my next album." The album happened to be *John Wesley Harding,* which, up until *Slow Train Coming,* was the most spiritual of all his albums.

"In the course of that two-hour talk, Dylan said, 'You're from Michigan, aren't you?' I said, 'Yes.' I was surprised that he remembered, although I remembered he was from Minnesota. And he asked, 'Are you going back there soon?' I said, 'Yeah, I do believe I am.' And he said, 'Well, go back there a little bit earlier than the concert and spend some time walking around.'

"That is a very bizarre thing to suggest. Almost like something a prophet would say. But I filed it away, and the next thing he asked was, 'Have you read the Bible?' And I said,

'No.' And he looked at me. It must have taken every ounce of kindness in his body at that point, but he just said, 'I think you ought to read the Bible.' Here I was, a guy who's asking what the secret of life is, and I hadn't read the handbook."

This conversation, along with Noel's growing spiritual openness, led to an interesting backstage encounter after a performance in Austin, Texas. Stookey was signing autographs and saw a young man watching him. He walked over and asked, "What is it you would like to talk to me about?" And the young man said, "I want to talk to you about the Lord."

Noel was initially a little guarded, but within a few minutes he sensed that the young man was honest. By that time Noel was very interested in learning about having a relationship with God. The young man had two friends with him, and the four of them went to a motel to talk. The first thing the young man said was "I think we ought to pray." The young man prayed with his friends for a while, and then said to God, "And now I think Noel wants to talk to you."

At first Noel was silent. "There was only me and the face of the One I had sought for so long. And I didn't know what to say, but I had a strong feeling that my first response should be to apologize and say, 'I'm sorry.' In the process of saying 'I'm sorry,' and in front of witnesses, I broke down crying.

"I think I see now that aside from the classic repentance, I was also repenting for having locked the presence of a real God out of my life for so long. And intermixed with 'I'm sorry' were 'Whew' and 'Boy!' It was like that for about a half an hour and then the kid laid hands on me and spoke in a language that must have been tongues, and I was different."

The next day Stookey was back on the road, on his way to the next Peter, Paul, and Mary concert. He wondered whether his experience the night before would affect his life in any lasting way. One thing he noticed was that he couldn't put down the Bible. He managed to do his two-hour performances every night but other than that, all he wanted was to be immersed in the Word.

He recalls, "Now I was reading the Bible from the perspective of someone who had been visited, and it took on a new significance. All the words seemed different. Instead of ancient history, I was reading about how someone related to a timeless God with whom I had a relationship and was having a relationship."

Now, in addition to his work with Peter, Paul, and Mary, Stookey also works solo and with Band and Bodyworks, where he performs many of his new faith-based songs.

■   ■   ■

Reading Scripture helped the people in this chapter make sense of history—the world's story. Applying that scripture personally helped them make sense of their own lives. As so many have discovered, a single passage in Scripture can simultaneously address the past, present, and future of the human race, and the past, present, and future of the reader.

Robert Bellah, the sociologist who edited *Habits of the Heart*, a study of the values that shape American life, has concluded that the modern, secular view finds the world intrinsically meaningless. Bellah advocates the recovery of biblical language in everyday life. He writes, "The texts are there, those great biblical texts, as alive and vibrant and sharp and pointed and relevant to our lives as they have ever been. But we must apply them."[13]

CHAPTER FIVE

Drawn to Community

The physical presence of other Christians
is a source of incomparable joy
and strength to the believer.

—Dietrich Bonhoeffer

Originally this chapter was titled, "Search for Community." But no one I interviewed actually said that they'd been looking for community. Quite a few people, though, were deeply attracted to Christian community when they found it.

This was good news to me. Christians understand that the church is a hospital for sinners, not a sanctuary for saints. But onlookers often have high expectations for Christians, which aren't always met. Jesus said that the world would recognize his followers by the love they show each other. He told his disciples to love each other the way he loved them—a high standard. So it was encouraging to hear about Christian communities that have shown the love and peace of Christ.

When Dietrich Bonhoeffer wrote the words quoted at the beginning of the chapter, he was savoring communal life in a seminary. But he was not able to enjoy that life for long. The seminary was part of the Confessing Church Movement in Germany—set up in opposition to the state church and Nazi policies regarding the Jewish people. The seminary was soon closed down. The Nazis arrested Bonhoeffer in April 1943 and executed him in April 1945, less than one month before the end of the war.

Bonhoeffer must have known what resistance to the Nazis might mean when he wrote these words: "It is easily forgotten that the fellowship of Christian brethren is a gift of grace, a gift of the Kingdom of God that any day may be taken from us, that the time that still separates us from utter loneliness may be brief indeed. Therefore, let him who until now has had the privilege of living a common Christian life with other Christians praise God's grace from the bottom of his heart."[14]

The Displaced Person ■ ■
Marian Konrad ■ ■

One of the most moving short stories I've ever read is "Amy Foster," written by Polish-born author Joseph Conrad (Korzeniowski). The story poignantly portrays the loneliness and alienation of an Eastern European immigrant living in a small English village. There are parallels in this story to the real-life story of Marian Konrad.

As is true with most Polish people, Marian was raised in a Catholic family. At the beginning of World War II, he was taken from his small Polish town and assigned to work as a slave for a Nazi who owned a brewery and a large farm in Austria.

At that time Austria was under Nazi authority, and the Nazis viewed Slavs as an inferior race. While in Austria, Marian approached the town's Roman Catholic priest with the hope of establishing a spiritual relationship. The priest responded that he could not take Marian under his care because he was Polish, and the Nazis had forbidden Polish and other Eastern European people from participating in religious services. This conversation stunned Marian, who asked himself, "Where is Jesus Christ?"

A few years later, Marian found himself in Rome, days after the city was liberated. Being Catholic, it was an opportunity to visit the Vatican and so he did. There were very few visitors to the Vatican and many sections were closed off, but that was the only indication of anything unusual. Marian recalls, "The streets of Rome were full of military activities, refugees, makeshift tents in city parks, and soup kitchens. None of that was visible in the Vatican, where the show of wealth seemed pompous and cold under the circumstances.

Again I asked myself, 'Where is Jesus Christ?' while the streets of Rome were begging for Christ." Marian remembers very clearly that this was the moment in his life that led him away from all organized religion and churches.

The war experience, witnessing many brutalities, and suffering from starvation and deprivations, left him with a hatred of Germans. At the close of the war, Marian found himself in Italy as a member of the occupation forces. One day he heard that a movie he wanted to see was playing in a nearby town. Fortunately he found a military truck that would take him and several others to the movie and pick them up later. Seated in the packed theater, he realized from their conversation that he was next to two Austrians. He got up and left the theater. Because it had been illegal for him to sit next to them in their own country, he refused to sit next to them now.

After the war, as part of the British forces, Marian was shipped to Glasgow, Scotland, where he married a Scottish girl. But as a Polish immigrant in Britain, he always felt like an outsider, and he and his wife eventually moved to California where his children were born. The children's mother had a Christian upbringing and wanted to provide the same experience for their children. Marian didn't object, but he didn't personally participate. As time went on, many of his children's activities were centered in a small community church. They participated in camp, skits, singing groups, and Sunday School. Marian found it difficult to turn down invitations to see what his children were learning and doing.

Soon, not only Marian's wife and kids but Marian himself looked forward to church on Sunday morning and to seeing his many new friends. On one of his first visits, one of the elders asked him if he was "saved." Not knowing what that meant, he said "Yes" to be, in his judgment, on the safe side. On the way home in the car he ask his wife what it actually meant.

Unlike his experiences of exclusion from worship in Austria and from community in Great Britain, Marian felt accepted in this small church. For the first time in his life, he was exposed to Biblical teaching. He discovered a wealth of knowledge and life-changing applications. "It was the first time that I understood that I could have direct communication with God," Marian remembers.

In this environment, Marian developed a hunger and thirst for Scripture and a desire to live a life that glorifies God. He discovered a deep sense of peace and a love of God's creation. One of the results of this life change was that Marian decided to let go of his resentment toward the German people, realizing that it was inconsistent with his new life and also that it "was killing me, not the Germans." Being surrounded by a caring Christian community made it easier for him to release old hatred.

Hearing the Word ■ ■
Kathleen Norris ■ ■

Kathleen Norris abandoned her faith when she went to Bennington College, a place where "psychiatry and the arts" substituted for religion. In that secular atmosphere, religion seemed like something she'd done as a kid but no longer had any use for.

After college, as a poet living in New York City, Kathleen was aware that poets like John Berryman, Anne Sexton, and Robert Lowell had explored religion but never quite connected with it and had been driven to breakdowns instead. At that point, religion seemed like an intriguing but potentially dangerous territory for a poet.

Kathleen had a close friend who studied theology and was reading theologians who were "demythologizing" Christianity—that is, taking out the supernatural elements. This friend was a scholar who had been heavily influenced by the German theologian Rudolph Bultmann. When Kathleen discovered a book by the Christian mystic Evelyn Underhill, her friend sneered at the idea of religious experience, telling her it was worthless. Kathleen felt that there was no place for her in the sterile religious world of her theologian friend.

Kathleen married another poet and lived for years in New York City. Then Kathleen and her husband decided to move to the prairie town of Lemmon, South Dakota, into a house she had inherited from her grandmother. As she sorted through her grandmother's things, including a hymnal and a Bible, Kathleen began reconsidering her own faith in the light of the Christian faith that had meant so much to her grandmother. Leafing through the old Bible, she read prayers that were written on pieces of paper and a printed sheet that advertised a preaching campaign of her grandfather's. Initially drawn to church for nostalgic reasons, eventually it became much more to her.

She says, "It was not an easy process or a conscious one for the most part. It just began to draw me. If there was so much in this religion for [my grandmother], it bothered me that I had been able to walk away from it. That struck me suddenly as not very bright, frankly, not right thinking."[15]

But like other baby boomers, Kathleen thought of religion as a repressive force, out to stop people from having fun.

"Only when I began to address that uncomfortable word, 'sin' did I see that I was not being handed a load of needless guilt so much as a useful tool for confronting the negative side of human behavior."[16]

Two communities drew Kathleen back to Christian faith. One was the Presbyterian church, her grandmother's church, just four doors down the street from where she was living. Kathleen feels that conversion is a necessity in a small, isolated town where you can't escape knowing your neighbors or being known by them. As she puts it, "The inner impulse toward conversion, a change of heart, may be muted in a city, where outward change is fast, noisy, ever present. But in the small town, in the quiet arena, a refusal to grow (which is one way Gregory of Nyssa defined sin) makes any constructive change impossible."[17]

The other community that nurtured Kathleen's conversion process was a Benedictine monastery about ninety miles from where she and her husband were living. After her first visit to the monastery, she dreamed about it every night for a week and understood that something significant had happened. She found a spiritual home with the hospitable Benedictines and visited them often. It was a place where she could sit and hear the Bible being read in a prayerful context. Over the period of a month, an entire book of the Bible might be read, and she learned a lot listening to the readings.

At some point during her conversion, under the influence of the Presbyterian and Benedictine communities that formed her past and present, Norris embraced the faith that had sustained her grandmother.

■ ■ The God Who Cares
■ ■ *Stephen Milozski*

By the time he was a teenager, Stephen Milozski had rejected the church he'd been raised in, which he felt offered formulas without much substance.

Later, when Stephen and his wife began searching for some kind of transcendence, something to give their life meaning, they didn't start with the church. They had tried drugs and decided that wasn't the right way. Then they were introduced to a yogic society that promised a lot of the things they were looking for. They were initiated, became strict vegetarians, and began looking for a truer spirituality through meditation.

Stephen and his wife had some strange experiences during meditation, but they didn't doubt the validity of the experiences because they were similar to ones described in ancient Eastern literature. They eventually moved to an ashram. When they began having problems in their relationship, they relied on their spiritual practices to shore them up. But meditation didn't solve their problems.

Eventually their marriage ended in a traumatic and painful breakup. Stephen was shattered, but when he turned to his community he found a complete lack of sympathy from other ashram members, who coolly explained his experience in terms of karma. To them, Stephen's problems were part of the illusion of life and didn't matter. In response to his agony, they exhorted Stephen to transcend the realm of material existence, which he attempted to do.

He describes his feelings at the time: "I wanted nothing more to do with anything at all in material existence. The only way of getting out, of getting off of the wheel of death and rebirth, of karmic existence was to meditate deeply and to attain *samadhi*—to find union with the absolute."

After a period of intensive meditation, Stephen felt that he had come into contact with the power of his guru, a man the ashram members regarded as God. But eventually he began having doubts. Stephen had been very impressed by an aphorism in the *Tao te Ching* by Lao-tsu who said, "Highest good is like water in that it excels in taking the lowest position." But this philosophy was totally at odds with the ashram's conception of spirituality, which advocated the use of physical and psychological force in the name of their guru, whom they believed would become the world ruler.

It was at this time that Stephen began to question whether the guru really was God incarnate. He says, "At 5:30 one morning a funny thing happened. I was taking my morning cold shower, and was in a great deal of turmoil, so I decided to go over the head of my guru and pray to God himself. It was strange because I found myself praying to Jesus. I prayed that if this guru was really Christ in the flesh, I would have it confirmed in my heart, putting my fears at ease. And if he wasn't, that he, Jesus, would help get me out."

Stephen was asked to become a trainer for the national organization, and then a scandal hit. Three of the people who had been in the organization the longest, who had gone to India several times and sat with the guru, became Christians after returning home. Since the group viewed Christians as part of a decadent spirituality and tools of an oppressive establishment, the conversions caused an uproar.

When these former yogis asked for a meeting, Stephen and others in his ashram agreed, thinking they could put their friends back on the right track. When Stephen first encountered one of them, he put his arm around him and said, "Well, what's filling your life these days?" And the man answered, "The love of Christ."

That shook Stephen up. "I began to realize that while I was looking for some sort of resolution to my predicament and to the human predicament in general, what I had accepted was dissolution of that predicament in my own private consciousness. I was looking for ultimate reality to speak for itself, but what I had accepted was a manipulation of consciousness that said ultimate reality was inside of myself. . . . The thing that really touched me about what these Christians said was that their portrayal of God was so far superior to anything I had heard or experienced."

Stephen went to a worship service with his old friends and found himself in such turmoil that he could hardly hear what the preacher was saying. What impressed him were the people in the congregation, who were singing and smiling and laughing and looking perfectly normal. They weren't distinguished by their dress or their actions, yet they seemed authentic. Stephen began praying that if God was real, he would make his reality known.

Several days later, Stephen and some friends from the ashram picked up a couple and a man in Eastern garb who were hitchhiking. The couple were Christians and began conversing with the man.

Stephen recounts what happened next as one of the strangest experiences of his life: "As they were talking, I began to see that the man was articulating all the questions I had about the relationship of Eastern mysticism to Christianity. A question would just form in my consciousness, and it would come out of this man's mouth. I realized what his question was at the precise moment he said it. This went on for about forty-five minutes straight.

"At that point, it was dawning on me that the odds of such a conversation taking place at all, much less taking place in front of me, were incalculable. It was impossible for that to have happened outside of the direct ordination of God. I started getting the impression that God really cared for me. He was interested in answering my questions in a way that I could see."

The next afternoon when the ashram went on a picnic, Stephen went off by himself to the top of a hill and began to pray the Lord's Prayer. "I prayed it, and it was like I had never prayed it before. It made such perfect sense to me. So much of my heart went into praying that prayer, and at one point I just began praising God and thanking Jesus.

"It was almost as though literal scales fell off my eyes. My perspective was changed, a 180-degree turnaround in a period of maybe eighteen hours. I was actually able to look at the world as God's creation, seeing the good in it, as opposed to looking at the world as illusion and trying to see through it. You can't imagine the freedom of being able to look at the world as really being there after years of conditioning yourself that it is not. At that point, I knew I was free with a freedom I had never before known existed."

A New Family ■ ■
Heather Weidemann ■ ■

Heather Weidemann grew up in New England. She went to a boarding school that was originally based on Christian values but, as she puts it, the doctrine had been "defanged." Years later she became a scholar of medieval and Renaissance literature. Once when she was teaching Milton at a university, some of her students witnessed to her and to their classmates. But Heather's image of Christianity was based on the public face of television evangelism, and it was something she wanted nothing to do with.

Heather went through an especially hard time with her own family. It was emotionally difficult "like a long slow dying that I was powerless to stop." The culmination came when she received a letter from her parents saying that they now felt estranged from Heather.

Heather had a lot of "intellectual pride" and had been fiercely independent. But later, when she had children, she found herself in need of a nanny, and she hired a Mien woman named Muang. Being dependent on a caregiver was humbling, and at first Heather found it difficult to surrender control.

Muang, though, turned out to be a jewel. The Mien are one of several Southeast Asian hill tribes recruited by the CIA during the Vietnam War to fight the communists. In the war's aftermath, they fled the country. Leaving their homes in Laos, the Mien escaped into Thailand where they were put into refugee camps.

The Mien are animists who believe that their gods demand sacrifice, and so they ritually offer the gods chickens and other items. When the Mien found themselves in the refugee camp, they had nothing to offer their gods. They began offering them stones, but feared that the gods wouldn't be pleased by such meager offerings.

One day some Christian missionaries came to their camp and told them about a God who didn't want their sacrifices, who had sacrificed himself for them. Many of the Mien became Christians at that time. When one of Muang's daughters became seriously ill, some Christians prayed for her and she was miraculously healed. As a result, Muang and her family became Christians.

As Heather found herself and her family under Muang's loving care, the two women became friends. In Laos, the Mien subsisted as rice and opium farmers, and they found adjustment to American life extremely difficult. Eventually Muang asked Heather if she would help a group of Mien women with their English language skills and invited her to a "Women of Jesus" potluck that they were having.

Heather says, "It was at this meeting that I first came to realize what it would mean to be in relationship with these people. I felt that something completely disruptive had come into consciousness for me. The group was very prayerful, and there were a lot of layers of emotion. But there was a third presence in the room. I felt like I was talking to someone in my head.

"I said, 'What do you want from me? What am I supposed to do?' Then I thought, 'Who am I talking to?' And something said, 'You need to get involved with these people. I want you to love the world more than you do now.' The Mien women wanted me to make a heart connection and something or someone else did too. But I didn't know if I could do it."

The Mien drew Heather into the heart of their community. She taught them English and counseled them through personal crises. She played baseball with them, started quilting projects with them, and worshiped with them.

Eventually she was adopted by members of a Mien clan and was given a Mien name. A Mien friend told her, "I'm born three times. I'm born to my mother in a jungle in Laos, I'm born to Jesus in the refugee camp where people were dying, and I'm born again when I came to America and I had to start my life all over again."

Heather feels that she is as much in need of God's healing as the Mien are, and that God ministers through them to her as well as from her to them. Because of the loss of her birth family, she deeply identifies with their loss of origin.

She also grew to share their experience of a God who does not abandon us in the face of loss. "In the process of becoming a Christian, I found myself arguing with God a lot, and I guess it was then that I knew that I was really part of a family. But there are still times when I would almost trade everything in my life for a mom and dad who loved me and saw me as a whole person. But God is faithful and came to me and made a way for me when there was no way. I have the Mien, and I have my church family too."

One of the things Heather has discovered about the Mien is that, uniquely among the Southeast Asian hill communities, they are an adopting tribe. They traditionally take in the cast-off or abandoned children from other tribes and raise them as their own. Heather's adoptive family has given her two Mien names. The first means "fourth daughter"—her adoptive family already had three daughters. The other name means "mother/teacher," which she sees as a reminder that she's not to remain a child but is called to grow up in God's family. Heather has come to believe that the community of believers, God's family, is also an adopting tribe.

She says, "There is a verse that means a lot to me—John 14:18. It's a promise Jesus makes to the disciples. He says, 'I will not leave you as orphans. I will come to you.' I love this verse because it's the one that first broke my heart open to God when I read it, and I love it because it is a promise that God wants to include all of us in his family. The biggest gift that God has given me is the gift of family."

■   ■   ■

Contemporary America is arguably the most individualistic society in world history. Yet we the people who make up this society long to be in a relationship. Turning to God is a matter of individual choice. But when we make this decision, we're reborn into a new family. As the people in this chapter discovered, community is a place where we are revealed, welcomed, and drawn into a new life together.

Theologian John G. Stackhouse has put it aptly: "Here are the two best ways to get our neighbors to take the gospel seriously: love them well. And love each other well. . . . The Christian gospel isn't fundamentally about changing to a new metaphysics or ethics or aesthetics. It's about changing families."[18]

CHAPTER SIX

Who Do You Say I Am?

In this divine love Jesus was sent
into the world, to this divine love
Jesus offered himself on the cross.

—Henri Nouwen

I recently read a *New York Times* review of a book called *A World Full of Gods: The Strange Triumph of Christianity*. This book describes the competing religious movements of Paul's day and asks why Christianity survived the rest of them. The author offers a few reasons. But the *Times* reviewer found the answers unsatisfying and concluded, "That's it . . .?"

With the whole pantheon of Greek and Roman gods to choose from, why join a religion that would lead to social ostracism, persecution, and death? To believers the answer is clear: Jesus himself. Without understanding who Jesus is, the ascendancy of Christianity from a small Jewish Messianic cult makes no sense.

During his public ministry, when more and more people were coming to hear him preach and to witness miracles, Jesus asked the disciples who people thought he was. They answered, "'Some say John the Baptist, but others Elijah, and still others Jeremiah or one of the prophets.' He said to them, 'But who do you say I am?' Simon Peter answered, 'You are the Messiah, the son of the living God.' (Matthew 16:14–16).

The question Jesus asked, "Who do you say I am?," is one that every person in this book had to answer during his or her conversion process. It's a question that each one of us needs to answer.

Cultural historian Jaroslav Pelikan has written: "Regardless of what anyone may personally think or believe about him, Jesus of Nazareth has been the dominant figure in the history of Western culture for almost twenty centuries. If it were possible, with some sort of super-magnet, to pull up out of that history every scrap of metal bearing at least a trace of his name, how much would be left? It is from his birth that most of the human race dates its calendars, it is by his name that millions curse and in his name that millions pray."[19]

I Can't Even Say His Name ■ ■
Beverly Liberman ■ ■

Beverly Liberman was raised in a religious Jewish home. Her family went to a conservative temple, observed the holidays, and kept kosher. Her devout father taught her Hebrew. When she was still a little girl, she sat with him on Friday nights and translated the five books of Moses from Hebrew to English.

As a child, Beverly definitely believed in God and talked to him. "I absolutely had no doubt that there was a God who lived up in the sky somewhere and looked like an old man. But even as a little girl I had a problem with hypocrisy. There was an emphasis in our house on living by the rules, and yet anybody who wasn't Jewish was slandered and slammed. I really had a problem with that."

Beverly's mother and her family fled Hitler's Germany. Beverly's father, who was at the American Embassy in Berlin, was able to get her family to the United States and was revered because of this. He was very religious, and Beverly tried hard to stick by all the rules to make him happy. But she found herself breaking them without meaning to.

For eight days during Passover, the dishes were put away and special Passover dishes were brought out. There were different milk dishes and meat dishes, and you weren't supposed to eat anything with flour in it.

"One day during Passover, I went over to my girlfriend's house to play," Beverly recalls. "Her mother offered me chocolate chip cookies and milk. I was sitting there playing jacks and eating, and all of a sudden it hit me. And that kind of thing happened to me all the time. As hard as I tried, I couldn't keep to the rules. So that's how I grew up—seeing the hypocrisy and knowing that I couldn't live up to the rules no matter how hard I tried."

As an adult, Beverly and her husband went to temple on high holidays but weren't particularly religious. Beverly was not happy with her life, and she began searching for answers. She joined a group of people who were into things like auras and reincarnation and taught that people keep being reborn until they reach Christ consciousness.

Beverly says, "I could deal with Christ consciousness because it was not Jesus, but I could not deal with Jesus. I grew up in an anti-Christian house where you did not talk about him. My mother blamed the holocaust on Jesus; it was irrational, but she did."

A member of her New Age group recommended that Beverly visit a psychic, so she did. But when she saw that there were pictures of Jesus all over the psychic's house, she became very uncomfortable. The psychic did a reading and told Beverly to buy a Bible in a modern translation and read one of the four gospels.

Beverly was open to trying new things, so she went to the UCLA bookstore and bought *The New English Bible*. She flipped through the gospels and finally settled on the book of Mark and read through it. She says, "All I remember was that Jesus kept calling the Jews hypocrites. So I threw up a little prayer and said, "OK, God, if this Jesus is someone for me, you're going to have to do something here because I can't even say his name unless I'm swearing."

Then some people from her group went to a Pentecostal church in Van Nuys. They came back and said they'd been baptized in the Holy Spirit. They had a special language they prayed in, and they asked Beverly whether she'd like to pray in this language too.

Beverly said, "OK, why not?" She had no idea what they were talking about, but says, "They prayed for me, and I did start talking in a language. And then one of them invited me to a Bible study, and it was there that I really heard the gospel for the first time.

"If I'd ever heard the gospel before I don't remember it. But the spirit of truth entered me, and then I could hear it. I started going to church and was just starved to know more. I gave my life to the Lord and was baptized. For five or six months I was very involved, and then I started being upset by the legalisms of the Pentecostal church. I felt that I was back in the legalisms of Judaism."

Meanwhile Beverly's family was very upset by her conversion. Her husband was furious. He told her, "I'd rather that you'd had an affair than that you do this." So she stopped going to church, but she never stopped believing.

Years later, when she moved to San Francisco, Beverly prayed, "God, please send me Christian fellowship and Christian friends." Then she met a woman who invited her to a Bible study, and through that group she found a church home.

As Beverly studied the Bible, she found her worldview changing. She says, "I was a vice president at Tiffany's. I'd been so driven to make lots of money and have the title. But I wasn't feeling purposeful; the title and the money didn't mean anything to me anymore. Every day I passed homeless people on the way to work, and it was starting to bother me. I would lie in bed at night under my down comforter and worry about how the homeless people were keeping warm."

Beverly ended up leaving Tiffany's and starting an organization to help the homeless, which is another story. But as she says, "It was a pretty radical change. And it happened because God was working in my life."

■ ■ An Academic Understanding
■ ■ *Maria Wright*

As an undergraduate, Maria Wright took a course entitled "Religion in Antiquity" and was fascinated when the professor insisted that the Greeks and Romans really believed in their gods. Previously she'd always thought that religion was something that happened on the sidelines. But this course led Maria to seriously consider what piety meant, what being devout meant.

She wondered, "If people were really so strong in their trust in the various gods of the pantheon, why did Christianity take such a hold? What was it that touched people?" But she asked her questions from a totally objective point of view. "I truly was not personally considering the Christian faith, not one bit. I wondered what marketing feature of Christianity made it something that people were willing to abandon their other religions for. If they had this trust in the Greek and Roman gods and it was so embedded in their political and social life, why did it get dropped? Academically I never really came up with a satisfactory answer."

She wondered whether the Christian view of the afterlife was more pleasing or soothing, or whether the sense of community that Christianity offered was more attractive. Then she thought, maybe Christianity took over because the emperor became a Christian and made it the state religion.

Finally Maria began to entertain the idea that perhaps there was some inherent truth in Christianity. Knowing that this question wasn't addressed within the academic world, she decided to study ancient religion from a theological perspective. Since classicists don't really teach religion from this view point, she was advised to go into theological studies. Maria entered Harvard Divinity School's program in History of Early Christianity and managed to get through nearly three years of their program almost never reading the Bible. But she did gain a deep interest in archaeology.

One of her closest friends at Harvard came from a conservative Christian background. She was Maria's first friend who was a serious believer who was also doing historical studies. Maria says, "That fascinated me and poked at me, but not enough to do anything about it."

Maria finished the master's program and decided that doctoral studies in Berkeley were the next step. She knew that for many other people in the world Christianity was a faith matter and decided to look at that perspective. But it was a head decision. She says, "I'd always had conversations with God, but never really engaged the faith questions. Particularly the question of Jesus; for me that was a real struggle."

When Maria started teaching, she encountered people who read the Biblical texts for inspiration or devotion. She could accept other people's faith, and even admire them, but she continued to avoid the Jesus question in any personal way. The academic work became her excuse for not engaging the issue on a faith level.

She was attracted to the community at First Presbyterian Church of Berkeley, where she took the Alpha course, an informal introduction to the Christian faith. No one in that group knew Maria was an academic so she felt free to be herself and say things like, "I just don't get the cross or the idea of having a personal relationship with Jesus." She says, "I tried to understand who Jesus was, why he was here, what his role was. I was really lost. I had to learn to let God speak to me through the text."

Archaeology can often be a testing ground for the Christian faith. Some archaeologists don't even accept the historicity of the Bible. But to Maria, archaeology bore witness to the fact that ancient people had faith and sacrificed much because of it. Archaeology brought her back to questions about Jesus.

Maria says, "I yearned for faith, and at the same time part of me was very resistant to it. My biggest challenge was trying to integrate my faith side with my academic side because they'd been so separate. I've come to appreciate the Bible as something more than mere historical text—there's a message in it. But it's very difficult to demonstrate the legitimacy of faith in the academic world. I think that the two sides come together quite well, but the environment simply doesn't support that."

It was during this intellectual struggle that Maria went through a personal crisis. "I had always made my way through the world with myself as Lord." She says, "I thought that I could work everything out. But then, despite all my best intentions, I created a path of destruction and ended up hurting several people who were very close to me.

"At that moment of crisis, I realized that I was completely helpless and alone. For the first time, I cried out in prayer and found myself asking Jesus for help. That's what shocked me the most. All this time I'd been resistant and never prayed to Jesus; I always prayed to God. Now it just slipped out of my mouth in a way that completely surprised me. Yet at the same time it seemed so natural."

For the first time, Maria understood what it meant to have a personal relationship with Christ, a phrase that had bothered her in the past. She says, "I had a sense of being embraced by somebody who is much stronger and wiser than me. Someone who is nurturing and is saying 'It's OK. I can take care of this.' Since having that experience, I have called myself a Christian."

None but Jesus Heard Me ■ ■
Sojourner Truth ■ ■

Many of us know Sojourner Truth as the freed slave whose eloquent, passionate speeches fueled both the abolitionist and women's rights movements in the United States. After fighting hard for African Americans to become voting citizens, she wasn't about to be disenfranchised because she was a woman.

One of her most famous speeches was given at the Akron, Ohio Women's Rights Conference in 1851. A number of men had been speaking out against women's rights, some implying that women were too delicate to assume such rights and, instead, needed to be protected by men. This was too much for Sojourner, who had never been pampered in her life. This was her reply:

That man over there says that women need to be helped into carriages, and lifted over ditches and to have the best place everywhere. Nobody ever helps me into carriages, or over mud puddles, or gives me any best place! And ain't I a woman? Look at me! I have ploughed and planted, and gathered into barns, and no man could head me! And ain't I a woman? I could work as much and eat as much as a man—when I could get it—and bear the lash as well! And ain't I a woman? I have borne thirteen children and seen them most all sold off to slavery and when I cried out with my mother's grief, none but Jesus heard me! And ain't I a woman?[20]

Sojourner Truth was born into slavery in 1797 in Ulster County, New York, and was named Isabella Baumfree. Although she received very little religious instruction, Isabella always prayed to God about the hardships she suffered as a slave. Once, when she heard that her former master was visiting the new family she was with, she decided to return with him because she preferred her life there. Although he told her she couldn't return, she packed a bag and approached his carriage. As she did so, she heard God's voice tell her that he was everywhere, that he pervaded the universe. She was so stunned that she barely noticed the carriage driving away.

Isabella took this message as a rebuke from God. Remembering unkept promises she had made to him, she now felt too vile to approach him. She longed to talk to God but felt that the gap between them was too large. She wished that someone would speak to God for her.

Then one day someone came to her, appeared to her in a vision, someone who radiated holiness and love. 'I know you, but I don't know you. . . . Who are you?' was the cry of her heart, and her whole soul was in one deep prayer that this heavenly personage might be revealed to her and remain with her. At length, after bending both soul and body with the intensity of this desire, till breath and strength seemed failing and she could maintain her position no longer, an answer came to her saying distinctly, 'It is Jesus.' 'Yes,' she responded, 'It is Jesus.'[21]

In the past, Isabella had heard Jesus spoken of, but she thought that he was just an eminent man. Now she felt greatly loved by him and was no longer afraid to approach God. She was filled with joy and felt that he was her own special friend. When she heard others talk about him, she felt a sense of jealousy, afraid that if other people got to know him, she would be cast aside. One day she heard some people reading about Jesus and asked them whether he was married. "What!" she was answered, "God have a wife?" And that was how Isabella learned that her great friend and intercessor was the Son of God.

In 1827, when New York state outlawed slavery, Isabella was emancipated. She then moved to New York City and worked as a domestic in several religious communes. In 1843, in response to another vision, Isabella changed her name to Sojourner Truth and traveled throughout the Eastern seaboard, preaching "God's truth and plan for salvation."

She later met and worked with abolitionists, including William Lloyd Garrison and Frederick Douglas, and also became an ardent defender of women's rights. During the Civil War she carried donations of food to black soldiers. Once, when she went to give an encouraging speech to these soldiers, her reputation as an orator attracted a huge crowd of white people. Worried that the black soldiers had been pushed to the edges of the crowd, she returned later to address them. In the 1860s, she rode Washington, D.C., streetcars and argued that they should be desegregated. She spoke before Congress and two presidents. Her strong sense of God's calling gave her a confidence rare in any woman of her day, much less an uneducated black woman born into slavery. As a woman who daily talked with God, no man, whatever his earthly standing, could intimidate her.

■ ■ No Other Hope
■ ■ *Malcolm Muggeridge*

Malcolm Muggeridge was a well-known journalist and television commentator in England. During his long career he served as the editor of the English humor magazine *Punch* and wrote frequently for *Esquire* and many other publications. Later in life, he was the presenter for a number of documentary films.

Muggeridge was raised by adamantly agnostic parents. His father was a socialist who believed that through a redistribution of society's wealth a utopian paradise could be established on earth—a materialistic paradise that had no place for God.

When he was growing up, Muggeridge viewed Jesus as a fellow socialist, a radical who had thrown the money changers out of the temple, who had been killed by the ruling powers and hated by the elite. This version of Jesus had nothing to do with anything supernatural.

After attending Cambridge University and getting married, Muggeridge and his wife moved to Cairo, where he had a teaching post. It was in Egypt that he began his career as a journalist, working as a foreign correspondent.

Continuing in his father's intellectual tradition, Muggeridge believed in human perfectibility and the possibility of an earthly utopia. When the Russian revolution took place, Muggeridge welcomed it as a wonderful moment in history.

This idealism was severely tested when Muggeridge actually witnessed life in postrevolutionary Russia. He and his wife lived in the Soviet Union in the fall and winter of 1932–33, when he worked as a correspondent for the *Manchester Guardian* and was one of the first journalists to report on the Ukrainian famine.

Walking the streets of Moscow, Muggeridge's faith in an earthly utopia was shaken. Stalin's purges taught him a lesson: "What I had failed to notice was that when the meek pushed out the mighty and took their places, they were then the mighty. Of course; they behaved as such and soon became fit to be put down themselves."[22]

It was some years later, when he was in Israel filming a documentary for the BBC, that Muggeridge reconsidered his understanding of Jesus. Although he felt that most of the shrines and relics had little credibility, Muggeridge found himself seized by a "mystical certainty about who Jesus was." He became convinced that there really had been a man, Jesus, who was also God.

The cross came to have special significance for Muggeridge: "The cross for the first time revealed God in terms of weakness and lowliness, even, humanly speaking, of absurdity. . . . Standing before the cross, God's purpose for us is made blindingly clear, to love Him, to love our neighbor."

Contrasting his faith with all his former pursuits, Muggeridge said, "I have found on this earth no other truth than that of the cross, no other hope than that of the resurrection."[23]

In his later years, Muggeridge became a passionate critic of the media he had worked in for so many years (described in his autobiography, *Chronicles of Wasted Time*). He believed that the media was, at least partly, responsible for a serious erosion of the awareness of God.

In an interview late in his life, Muggeridge commented: "The absolutely most essential thing for human beings is to have an awareness of their Maker, God, and to see their own lives in time in relation to God and in relation to eternity. . . . The only possible way that men and women can be free is through God and through Jesus, too, because Jesus provided the possibility of a relationship in human terms with God."[24]

■　　■　　■

That Jesus of Nazareth actually lived, that his life dramatically changed those who knew him, and that he affected the course of world history are facts that are easily understood. These things could be said of other historical figures. That Jesus is still changing the lives of people today is more of a mystery—something those who don't know him have a harder time understanding.

My husband has a great interest in old buildings and the history that surrounds them. Once, on a trip north from Los Angeles to Berkeley, we took the time to visit a few California missions that were off the beaten path. Some missions, like the famous San Juan Capistrano, are in metropolitan areas and attract many visitors. Others remain more isolated.

One of these, reached by a dusty country road, seemed to be in the middle of nowhere. We saw no other people, but the doors were unlocked and small signs gave historical information. We entered a little museum with rooms showing what life had been like for the early Franciscan missionaries. Next to this building was a small, untended cemetery where graves of long-forgotten priests and their Indian converts were marked with simple wooden crosses.

When we walked into the chapel, it became clear that the mission still served a worshiping community. We were there in spring, a few weeks after Easter, and a large hand-printed banner on the wall proclaimed, "He is alive!" He *is* alive.

CHAPTER SEVEN

Bearing Witness

Your people shall be my people,
and your God, my God.

—Ruth 1:16

The word "gospel" means good news. And when you have good news, especially of ultimate importance, you want to share it with the people you care about.

On one *Seinfeld* episode, Elaine suspects that her boyfriend, Puddy, is a Christian, because when she borrows his car the radio is always set to Christian radio stations. When she questions him, he admits to being a Christian, which makes her mad. She's not mad because he's a Christian but because he never witnessed to her. "If you're a Christian," she says, "you should try to save me." He says, "But you don't believe in God." Elaine's point is that he does, but he doesn't care about her enough to talk about it.

One way of witnessing is verbal. After his own conversion, the apostle Paul went into marketplaces and publicly argued the case for Christianity to people worshiping a variety of idols and gods. In our time, many people have become Christians through the work of gifted evangelists like Billy Graham.

Some years ago I was at a Billy Graham rally in Lausanne, Switzerland, sitting in the press section. A Swiss journalist— thin, nervous, and chain-smoking Gauloises— was seated next to me. I wondered how Billy Graham's powerful, straight-shooting gospel message sounded to this man. As he grew more agitated, I decided that he didn't like what he was hearing. When Graham gave the altar call at the end of his sermon and people began streaming down the aisles, my neighbor also went forward to receive Christ. This was a lesson to me: I should have been praying instead of doing a bad job of mind-reading.

But witnessing is not always verbal. People can live in such a way that their character bears witness. Paul Tokunaga, a Japanese American, says that Asian Americans are highly relational and very interested in observing the way people behave. Paul himself came to faith after watching a Christian named Gary forgive someone who had treated him badly. Paul says, "As I reflected on Gary's response for several days, I was won over to Jesus. I so badly needed to be forgiven for my sins. But I also desperately needed to see that Christianity was real and that it made a radical difference. Gary—a white guy—was the 'word who became flesh' for me. Shortly after, I gave my life to following Jesus."

Witnessing can be low key, part of a developing friendship. In a conversation with his neighbor Lon, Ken Slater casually mentioned that he was going to paint his mother's house the next Saturday. The next Saturday morning Lon showed up at Ken's door with a paintbrush and just quietly worked with him all day.

A few months later Lon showed up at Ken's door with a Bible. He said, "I thought you might like to read this, and if you're going to read it, I'd start with the book of Matthew." Some months later, Lon invited Ken to church with him. Through this friendship with Lon and with several other Christians he met, Ken and his entire family eventually became Christians.

A New Lens

Mary Stewart Van Leeuwen

Mary Stewart Van Leeuwen was raised in the United Church of Canada. She comments now, "I don't know if that counts as having a religious background. I have always said that the one good thing about the United Church of Canada is that they never used the Bible to put me down as a woman, but that is because they never used the Bible for much of anything."

When Mary was in university, she didn't go to church; it just didn't interest her. Between degrees, she traveled to Zambia and ended up teaching in a school that was run by the Salvation Army. She admired the Salvationists but wasn't ready to make a commitment to them. She was going to work on a doctorate in psychology at Northwestern University and couldn't see how Christianity related to her intellectual work.

On a later research trip to Zambia, Mary met a missionary couple who ran a place called Yielding Tree Farm, an informal Christian study center in the bush, modeled after L'Abri in Switzerland. Under their influence, Mary began reading authors like Francis Schaeffer and John Stott, and had some of her intellectual questions answered. But she was in Africa gathering data, not looking for her soul.

During one conversation, the man directing the study center told Mary about events that had happened during the East Africa Revival, a movement that resulted in many thousands of conversions and many miracles. The man told Mary that in the middle of a prayer meeting, an elderly woman who had been blind in one eye suddenly stood up and said, "I can see in my blind eye. I can see in both eyes." This was not something the woman had been asking for—it just happened.

As Mary listened to this story she had a "gestalt switch" experience. "For some reason the story made me see things totally differently. All of a sudden I saw the whole organization of the universe as something that God is doing—that we are all God's creatures. I also realized that it was my responsibility to respond. It felt like scales had fallen off my eyes and I was looking at life through a new lens. That was a real turning point for me. After that there was no turning back."

After she became a Christian, Mary decided to be rebaptized in a Baptist church in Lusaka. The pastor preached that morning on the passage about Lydia, the seller of purple cloth in the New Testament church. He said Lydia was this smart ex-patriot woman, and they were about to baptize another smart ex-patriot woman. The church was filled with African students from the University of Zambia, probably three quarters of the congregation were students who came by bus. The pastor said it meant a lot to these students to know that people actually came to Africa to hear the gospel and become Christians. Normally Westerners came to Africa to evangelize rather than to be evangelized.

When Mary went back to Canada and started teaching at York University in Toronto, she ran into a group of scholars— Dutch Calvinists—at the Institute of Christian Studies. They were deeply involved in scholarship that promoted a Scripturally directed understanding of the world. This became Mary's intellectual home, and it was in the context of that community that she met her husband, Ray, an Old Testament scholar.

Witness of the Word ■ ■
William Everson ■ ■

In the 1950s William Everson was known as a leader of the Beat generation of poets. He was part of the San Francisco Renaissance, a group that included Robert Duncan and Gary Snyder as well as native New Yorkers, Jack Kerouac and Allen Ginsberg. Everson has also been called one of the foremost

Catholic poets of our time. For eighteen years Everson was a member of the Dominican order where under the name Brother Antoninus, he wrote his most profound poetry on Christian themes. But throughout his life, including his time in the order, Everson was strongly attracted to women, and when he left the Dominicans it was to marry.

Everson grew up in California's San Joaquin Valley, where his father was a printer and musician. In high school, he was an indifferent student but an avid reader. In college, he discovered the poetry of Robinson Jeffers, which inspired his own lifelong vocation as a poet. He married his high school sweetheart, planted a vineyard, and wrote poetry until the outbreak of World War II. Everson became a conscientious objector and was sent to do alternate service in a work camp in Oregon. When he returned home, he was devastated to learn that his wife had become involved with another man.

After his divorce, friends introduced Everson to Mary Fabilli, a woman who was to have a dramatic effect on his life. Fabilli was a poet and artist, and also a Catholic. To please her, Everson started going to church. As he attended he became interested in Christianity. He was especially influenced by reading St. Augustine's *Confessions*. Augustine's deep faith touched Everson. Like Augustine, Everson was an intellectual. There were other similarities, as Everson noted: "And, of course, his travail of life, the separation from a beloved woman, was my own."[25]

Under the influence of his mentor, Robinson Jeffers, a nature poet who was "ferociously anti-Christian," Everson had become a pantheist. Now he found his thinking shifting. Everson tells of the following experience at a midnight mass at St. Mary's Cathedral in San Francisco in 1948:

When the fir-smell reached me across the closed interior air of the Cathedral, binding as it did the best of my past and the best of my future, shaping for the first time that synthesis of spirit and sense I had needed and never found, I was drawn across, and in the smell of the fir saw it for the first time, not merely as an existent thing, but as a created thing, witness of the Word, the divine Logos, who made all earth, and me, a soul in his own image, out of very love.[26]

Everson now believed that his earlier pantheism had been confusing because nature "was presumed to be the source itself. Whereas Christianity is the medium between man and God, and this gives nature a sharper definition."[27]

But it was the encounter with Mary Fabilli that initiated this change in his perspective. Many years after his conversion, when Everson was poet-in-residence at Kresge College, at the University of California, Santa Cruz, he recalled: "It was the personal witness of an individual that made the difference. Before that I was not a nonreligious person—I was a pantheist—but when this woman moved into my life it was almost as if the abstract divinity in the cosmos of pantheism became personal. And it was this personal factor that led to Christ. When I could see God as individual from nature, the next step was seeing Christ as God."[28]

Taking the Water
Treena Kerr

Treena and Graham Kerr were living in an early nineteenth century mansion on the shore of Chesapeake Bay. Graham was a chef with a successful TV show, and Treena was the show's producer. One day a young black woman knocked at their door. She came from an inner-city Pentecostal Holiness church and said she wanted to go to Haiti to serve the poor.

Graham Kerr, who had answered the door, asked her whether she could speak Creole French or any kind of dialect. When she said, "No," Kerr asked how she was going to go over there and help people. She said, "I have a strong back, willing hands, and I've got Jesus in my heart." When she added, "My church is so small and they haven't got any money," Kerr braced himself to be solicited for a donation.

But instead the young woman, named Ruthie Turner, surprised Kerr by saying, "We were praying and decided that I should come to a big house in a wealthy area, and ask the people whether they wanted a maid and then I would work for them until I saved enough to go to Haiti."

That got to Kerr who also knew they could use some household help. And so the Kerrs hired Ruthie and paid her a good wage.

Soon after she began working for them, Ruthie realized that Treena Kerr was in serious trouble—she was angry and violent and taking a lot of pills. When Ruthie saw the condition Treena was in, she started praying. She went back to her church and told them about the woman in the big house on the hill. And they prayed for her too.

One day Ruthie said, "Mrs. Kerr, why don't you give your problems to God?" And Treena said, "OK, God, if you're there, you do something because I can't do any more." Ruthie then asked her whether she'd like to be baptized. And Treena said, "I'm from England, where everybody is christened at birth." Ruthie explained that taking the water meant dying to yourself and all your sins. Treena declined. But, Treena remembers, as Ruthie walked away, "This little voice said, 'What do you do when you've lost your temper?' I would always take a shower or jump in the swimming pool. So I called Ruthie back and said, 'OK, I'll take the water.'"

Ruthie arranged it all, and on the following Tuesday Treena drove out to Ruthie's church with her oldest daughter, Tessa, and Graham's secretary, Michelle. The church was in a little town called Bethlehem, and it was packed. They had come a hundred miles from Delaware to see this white lady who they'd been praying and fasting for get baptized.

The pastor asked, "Do you know what you're doing?" And Treena said, "I most certainly do." He said, "You may not get it tonight." And Treena said, "I most certainly will." (Whatever "it" was.) Then she changed into Ruthie's white baptismal gown and was put in the front row next to the peeling pale blue concrete tub under a naked light bulb.

People started praying. Treena wasn't used to praying. "But," she says, "when I shut my eyes, it felt like someone thumped me on the back and pushed me on onto my knees. As I hit the ground I heard myself saying, 'Jesus, I'm sorry. Forgive me, Jesus.' Well, I swore Jesus' name all the time. So to hear myself say something like that was quite astonishing. As I spoke, this water, and I can't call them tears, because it was more like rushing water, came out of my eyes. Then I got up and looked around to see who had pushed me. But everybody was singing with their hands in the air.

"The pastor asked me, 'Have you received it?' And I said, 'No, I don't think so, but something very strange happened just now.' Then I was put in this tub of water. It was December, and this sinner needed the icy cold water. So I got dunked, and when I looked up I saw all these beautiful African-American faces smiling at me."

After Treena got out of the water, the pastor asked her whether she'd like to tarry awhile. Treena said, "What's tarry?" And he said, "Waiting for the Holy Ghost." And Treena said, "Well, I might as well as I'm here." He said, "You just kneel down and thank Jesus for the gift he's going to give you." So she knelt down. Treena recalls saying, "'Thank you, Jesus' to someone I didn't believe in. Suddenly this bright light came on my face and, having been in the theater and knowing about entertainment, I thought, well they've turned the lights on to make me feel that I'm getting whatever 'it' was.

"Then I opened my eyes, and there standing in front of me was the most incredible, beautiful person I've ever seen with this loving, amused smile on his face. He put his hand on my heart and then disappeared. Then the pastor looked at me and asked, 'Have you received anything yet?' and I said, 'No, but I've just seen somebody.' He said, 'Never mind. You can come again.' So I got up and all these black brothers and sisters came and welcomed me to the flock."

When she got home, Treena pulled out the Bible that Ruthie had suggested she buy. For the first time, she didn't take sleeping pills before going to bed. Instead she got up and gathered all the medications she was on, threw them into the toilet, and pulled the chain on a rainbow of colored pills. Then she got into bed and started reading the New Testament for the first time.

Treena remembers, "I'll never forget it, it was like eating— like I'd been very hungry and I was stuffing the words in my mouth. I woke up with the Bible lying on the floor, and I felt great." Treena ran to the mirror to see whether she looked like

Ruthie, who always had a twinkle in her eyes, and when she looked in the mirror she saw life again in her own eyes. And she knew she had "it."

A Miracle ■ ■
Graham Kerr ■ ■

Graham Kerr had been out of town during the week of Treena's transformation so he had no idea that anything had happened.

When he came home, he immediately noticed a difference. Everything was fine—there were no shouts, no difficulties, just loving-kindness. Graham thought it must be because it was Christmastime, but the peace lasted beyond Christmas.

Then one day in a supermarket, a woman came up to Graham and told him that she had been baptized in the same way that his wife had. Graham was sure that the woman was confused, because he knew Treena had never done anything religious in her life.

But when Graham told Treena about the funny incident at the supermarket, she said that it was true. They sat on the floor in the middle of the room, and Graham said, "Well, what about reincarnation, what we've always believed in?" Treena said she didn't believe that anymore.

Graham asked Treena whether she wanted him to become a Christian, and she answered, "I don't know about you. I only know about me. But why don't you ask God about it yourself?"

In the weeks that followed, Graham watched Treena closely. This was a woman he had known since he was eleven, his first girlfriend. He recalls, "Here I was inspecting the woman whom I had loved all my life and whom I'd hurt terribly. I'd worked with her under enormously pressured circumstances and had failed her as a faithful husband. I personally took responsibility for having destroyed her. Now she was totally put back together again, and really happier and more loving than anytime I could remember."

Graham was impressed, but that made him think, "What about me?" He was in the middle of a very active career where he was lauded and idolized. He had a substantial income and yet had failed the one person he loved with all his heart. He had the kind of career he had hoped for and yet felt that in the whole of life he had failed.

Meanwhile Treena's doctor had come to see Graham and said, "Your wife is a miracle." His eyes filled with tears as he told Graham, "I believe in miracles. I had never seen one and now I have." Graham was moved by all of this too, but he still didn't know how to find God for himself.

The Kerrs had some big trees on their property, including an elm tree that was supposed to be the oldest tree in Maryland. So Graham went out and stood by the tree and said, "OK. God does miracles. If you're there, then I would like to know, please, whether you would do a miracle for me."

The tree didn't talk back or even tremble. But Graham is convinced that God did perform a miracle that day. The Kerrs had a really great house—something like Tara in *Gone with the Wind*—and Graham greatly valued the house as well as his other possessions.

But when Graham asked for a miracle and turned from the tree to go back to the house, everything changed. He says, "All the manufactured lights went out in all the things I owned. I was discontented with the house, the cars, boats, career, clothes, gold watch, everything. I didn't want replacements either."

Graham remembers, "For thirty days, I was without any god. The god for whom I worked so hard had been materialism, and now I didn't have Jesus or Mammon either." During this time Graham went on trying to work without any motivation; all he saw was the absolute slavery of it all.

Finally, he was so desperate for a relationship with God that he fell on his knees in a hotel room in Canada and began shouting to the ceiling: "What do I have to say to you to get to know you the way Treena does?" Treena had become radiant. And their children who had been broken and wounded were all back home and "all loving Treena and Treena was loving them, and I was on the outside." Graham says, "The next words I spoke were these: "Jesus—I love you." I heard myself saying words I could scarcely imagine myself saying. I was a 190-pound egomaniac at the time.

"I experienced an immediate and extraordinary wave of awareness; it was a perfect blend of joyful anticipation and real peace. I was free both to love and be loved . . . to be a friend and to have a friend."

■　　　　■　　　　■

An interesting movie called *Witness* came out a few years ago. It tells the story of a young Amish widow (Kelly McGillis) who goes on a train trip with her young son. In a Philadelphia train station, the boy witnesses a murder. In an attempt to solve the murder and protect the witness, a police detective (Harrison Ford) travels to the woman's home. A romance develops between the widow and the detective, despite the enormous differences in their cultures—the violent inner city world of the policeman and the simple farming community of the Amish.

As the story unfolds, the title *Witness* takes on a double meaning. The young boy is a witness to an event, in this case a crime. But his mother's character bears witness to the peaceful habits of the Amish (an Anabaptist Christian sect).

There are two ways the people in this chapter are witnesses also. They witnessed an event, Christ's advent in their own lives. And through their words and lives, they witnessed to others.

CHAPTER EIGHT

Broken Relationships

It's not possible for someone
to interact with a fellow human being
without leaving some traces.

—Shusaku Endo in *The Girl I left Behind*

Humans were created to be in relationship with God. We're made in the image of a triune God—even within the Godhead there are three persons. God created humans to have fellowship with him, and God created Eve for Adam because it wasn't "good for man to live alone."

Our social structures and personal relationships form the way we view ourselves. A break in those relationships can shake us up, undermine our confidence, and make us question the world and our place in it.

This chapter includes stories of people who had a close relationship severed through divorce, abandonment, or death. In each case the person went through a shift in consciousness that led to a relationship with God.

■ ■ Ultimate Reality
■ ■ *Phillip E. Johnson*

Phillip Johnson was raised in a nominally Christian family. He grew up in the Midwest, where going to church was something good kids did, like joining the Boy Scouts or Girl Scouts. Phillip's mother took him and his sister to Sunday school and dropped his father off at the golf course on the way. This left Phillip with the impression that "when you're a grown-up and your mother can't tell you what to do anymore, you play golf on Sunday."

Phillip believes that he absorbed something from his early years in Sunday school because through his young adult life as an "agnostic," he was really "a largely passive inquirer." He wasn't hostile to the Christian gospel. In fact, he read all of C. S. Lewis's books and was intrigued by them. But he thought Christianity was for another time or another kind of person, not for contemporary intellectuals like him.

Phillip was always a gifted academic. He entered Harvard after his junior year in high school, and he graduated first in his class at the University of Chicago law school. He says now, "That sort of success leads to intellectual and spiritual pride." He thought he didn't need the kind of things that ordinary people need, and that attitude became a barrier to accepting Christ.

All the while, Phillip thought Christianity was intellectually interesting—that he ought to look into it, but from a safe distance. He says, "I was a genuine inquirer but one who is always putting his toe in the water without ever considering jumping in."

He became a law professor at the University of California in Berkeley, got married, had a family, and rarely thought about Christianity. His life was in good order. He was happily married and enjoying family life. He had the kind of career he wanted and expected to go on to other prestigious positions and become "some kind of big shot in the legal world." But then his marriage abruptly ended, bringing pain and self-doubt. A difficult period of single parenting followed the breakup, "proving to me that I wasn't as good a parent as I had thought."

At the same time Phillip began to find his professional life as a legal scholar unsatisfying. He was writing papers that didn't mean much to him and didn't have a huge audience. Although he was superficially successful and was promoted within the university, he felt that he'd missed the point of life. Phillip says, "With this new perspective I finally got over my intellectual pride and was able to say 'I'm just like everybody else and I need the same things they do.'"

Shortly before the breakup, Phillip's daughter was attending a vacation Bible school and needed a parent to go with her to the closing-night event. Her mother wouldn't go because she was in active rebellion against her own conservative upbringing. So Phillip had volunteered to go. It turned out to be the same week that his wife told him she was leaving.

Phillip and his wife had agreed to tell the children about the split that weekend, and Phillip was going to tell his daughter right after the church program on Friday night. So it was with "a great deal of heightened awareness" that he heard the pastor, Bill Beatty, preach the gospel that night. Phillip doesn't remember what the pastor said. But he does remember thinking, "This man really believes what he's saying and lives his life by it, and I could too."

Even though nothing decisive happened that night, Phillip went from being a passive inquirer to actively considering becoming a Christian. It wasn't a "blinding light" conversion but rather a process of gradually being drawn into the body of Christ. Friends brought Phillip to the First Presbyterian Church of Berkeley where he met his second wife. Phillip says he wasn't dragged kicking and screaming into the Kingdom but was "drawn by the gentle and persistent and irresistible flow of a current."

He recalls, "I found a new life. I still had to work through my problems. It wasn't so much that I had help dealing with a particular problem. Rather, for the first time, I had a glimpse of a light at the end of the tunnel—which is to say, the real meaning of life and how I might fit into ultimate reality. It was more thrilling than the solution to any particular problem or set of problems."

At first Phillip found himself uncomfortable with the

teaching at church. As he listened, he realized that the academic world he belonged to was proceeding on entirely different assumptions.

He says, "The non-Christian world operates on modes of thinking that are fundamentally different from the Christian ones. The difference is not superficial, and it isn't bridgeable by the conventional remedies—the two ways of thinking are fundamentally opposed. That realization led me to a course of intellectual work that resulted in the five books I've written."

A Cult of One ■ ■
Peggy Vanek-Titus ■ ■

Although Peggy Vanek-Titus spent time in her early twenties in a Christian community, she had a basic problem with Christianity that took her years to resolve—she didn't believe in sin. She was young and idealistic when she first heard the gospel, and the idea that people were sinful was repellent to her. And since she believed that people were basically good, the idea that Jesus died for our sins made no sense to her.

Yet she was very drawn to this Christian community and trusted the people in it. During the time she spent there, she felt protected. She knew she was supposed to have a personal relationship with Jesus and could have "spouted off" about it, but she also knew it was something that she didn't have. Although she was accepted into the group, she secretly felt that there was a chasm between her and the others.

She had gone through a very rebellious adolescence, but did believe in God. At one point she prayed, "Well, I guess I've done just about every rebellious thing I could do. But please, God, never, never let me go no matter what." It was a sincere prayer that she felt God has honored over the years, though her life would take many turns before she came back to him.

As she grew older and experienced pain and suffering, Peggy came to believe in the reality of sin in the world and the need for redemption. She joined a Bible study and began to reconnect with God. At the same time she was going through a family crisis and was working on some related issues with a therapist. It was during this vulnerable period that she met Michael, the love of her life.

She soon quit the Bible study, left therapy, and focused all her attention on this new man in her life. He was handsome, charming, and successful. Looking back on it, Peggy says she abdicated her life to him. Her relationship with Michael mirrored many of her unresolved family issues. She looked to him for approval and affirmation, always wanting to prove that she was good enough for him. She says now, "He became my idol; I worshiped him."

Peggy's relationship with Michael lasted eight years, and during that time they were twice engaged to be married. Each time he changed his mind shortly before the wedding. Peggy says, "I never chased him, but whenever he came back into my life I made myself available." Each time Michael pulled away from her, Peggy suffered a loss of self-esteem and wanted another chance to prove herself.

When Michael finally walked out of her life for good, Peggy went through a long period of grieving and then felt an enormous sense of relief. She felt that she had mercifully been delivered from a damaging relationship. She says now that she had created "a cult of one." Breaking up with Michael felt like leaving a cult, like starting life over again.

She ended up reconnecting to God and in that relationship found the acceptance that Michael had never given her. She'd made it a point of honor to reveal her flaws to Michael, but he rejected her. With God, Peggy found she could be completely honest without fear of abandonment. A passage in Ephesians inviting her to "come boldly before the throne of worship" made Peggy weep. She'd finally found the affirmation she'd needed for such a long time.

A Softer Heart ■ ■
Diane Smith ■ ■

Diane Smith had been staunchly anti-Christian for much of her life, since about the age of fourteen. By the time she was in her late twenties, she felt that most Christians were hypocritical, smarmy, and not very bright. Yet at the same time, her life was flat. She was just going through the motions—going to work and coming home and feeling very lonely.

Then Diane's grandmother, who was the only Christian in the family, became seriously ill. At another time Diane would have mocked Christianity, but as her grandmother approached death from cancer, Diane bought her what she thought was a devotional book. It was the *Women's Devotional Bible,* and it was meant to be a Christmas present.

But her grandmother died before Christmas, leaving Diane with this Bible sitting in her house. A couple of weeks after her grandmother's funeral, the Gulf War broke out. Normally Diane would have been out in the streets protesting the war. But instead she found herself sitting in her apartment watching the war and the riots in San Francisco on TV and thinking, "This stuff has been going on forever, and these people marching in the street aren't solving anything."

She began asking questions about how the world worked, because it certainly wasn't working the way she thought it should. One day she opened the Bible and started reading in Genesis. Diane recalls, "Because Grandma had just died, my heart was much softer than it had been in a long, long, long time.

"Normally when I came home from work, I immediately wanted noise—so I'd turn on the TV, make myself something simple for dinner, and while away the evening. But now I couldn't turn on the TV or, if I did turn it on, it would not even register. My attention was being focused elsewhere. For a period of about five months, I read the Old Testament in the morning and the New Testament in the evening."

Reading about the Passover and the scapegoat lamb in the morning made sense of what she read in the evening about Christ being crucified. She says, "The image of the sacrificial lamb and the image of Christ merged in a way that I can't really explain."

Diane started going to a Wednesday night Bible study at a church she'd chosen because of its architecture. She can remember praying to God, "Please show me someone who will help me understand what I'm reading and what I'm thinking, and help me understand You better." And she had one particular person in mind.

The man who ended up helping her was not the one she wanted. Diane remembers, "This man was someone I had been put off by; he seemed coarse and loud. But I ran into him one night, and we ended up spending the next two hours together while he answered questions for me. I thought that was pretty funny; that God would use the one person I did not want." At church, new relationships were forming and she was learning at a very rapid pace.

But at work things were more difficult. Diane had been known for her witty and cutting remarks, but now she began fighting her sarcasm. At times she bit her tongue just to keep her mouth shut. Her relationships were changing, but there was still a lot of tension between her and her boss.

She walked into his office early one day and told him, "I realize that we haven't been getting along, and I just wanted to tell you that I'm sorry." That was all she said but he listened to her, and after that the relationship changed. Things got much better.

The rest of her life was flourishing. A woman she met discipled Diane and gave her a strong foundation for her new life with Christ. Diane was starting to feel healthier and when she looks back at her journals, the pre-Christ journal seems very angry. She says, "It's filled with my anger about all the relationships in my life—with friends, coworkers, and family members. The post-Christ journal was more about asking questions and recording this journey I was going on. It's pretty striking to look at the difference between those two journals and realize that it was all about being healed."

■   ■   ■

Over the years, as I've reviewed scores of movies for *Radix* and other publications, I've found that films dealing with spiritual life are rare. Films about Christian conversion are even rarer.

Christian faith concerns the heart's relationship with God —which is difficult to convey visually. But it's not impossible.

One of the best conversion movies I've ever seen is *The Mission,* which begins as a story of broken relationships. The movie stars Robert DeNiro as Mendoza, a Spanish slave trader in South America in the 1500s. Returning from a trip, Mendoza finds that his fiancée and his brother are having an affair. In a jealous rage, he kills his brother in a sword fight.

At that point, he's lost the two people in the world that he was closest to. In addition, he carries an enormous sense of guilt for his brother's death. In his anguish, he asks a priest for some kind of penance. The priest tells him to join an expedition to help a remote tribe of Indians. In addition to the priest's penance, Mendoza makes up his own. He carries a huge burden of armaments on his back through the rugged jungle.

When the missionaries struggle up an especially steep cliff, Mendoza is in danger of dying if he doesn't let go of his burden. But he won't let go. Suddenly, one of the Indians rushes over and cuts him free, and Mendoza sobs in relief. It's a great moment. It's also a wonderful symbol of God's offer to free us from our burden of sin and guilt and to heal our brokenness.

CHAPTER NINE

The Hound of Heaven

Lord, with what care hast thou
begirt us round? . . .
Fine nets and stratagems to catch us in,
Bibles laid open, millions of surprises,
Blessings beforehand, ties of gratefulness,
The sound of glory ringing in our ears.

—George Herbert

Jesus told his disciples that he is the good shepherd who gives His life for His sheep. This is a comforting image for those of us who want God in our lives—we will not be forgotten but will always be in God's care.

But for people who aren't looking for God, or are trying to escape God, the hound of heaven pursuing them through time may be a more apt image. The phrase comes from the title of a poem by Francis Thompson. In it, a man who desperately wanted to evade the hound went to the edges of the universe where he "troubled the gold gateways of the stars." But even there he was found.

The phrase "hound of heaven" has become a familiar part of English usage, sounding slightly archaic, with resonances of hunting parties in the English countryside. But at the time the poem was published, its influence was profound. G. K. Chesterton called it an event of history as well as of literature, and called Thompson a great poet.

Francis Thompson's poems might never have been written or read. His father, a medical doctor who wanted his son to follow in his footsteps, sent Thompson to medical school. But Francis, who loved literature, wasn't cut out for medical studies. He quietly dropped out of school and then out of sight altogether. He developed a drinking problem, became addicted to opium, and eventually found himself destitute—living on the streets of London.

Thompson wrote poetry in a public library until he was asked not to return because he was too ragged. But in the library he had seen a new Catholic magazine called *Merry England,* and in 1888 he sent some poems to the editor, Wilfrid Meynell, giving a post office as his address. Meynell wanted to publish the poems as soon as he read them and immediately wrote to Thompson, but the letter was returned. Meynell published the poems anyway. Thompson saw them in the magazine and made contact again, this time giving the address of a pharmacy. When the editor went to the pharmacy, he found the poet outside selling matches, trying to pay off a large debt for opium.

Meynell paid off Thompson's debt, bought him food and clothing, and arranged for him to stay in a monastery where he received medical treatment and kicked his habit. Thompson then moved near a Franciscan priory in north Wales where he continued to write more poetry. Sadly, he died of tuberculosis at the age of forty-eight. But he had gained the solace he described at the end of his most famous poem:

> Shade of His hand, outstretched caressingly?
> Ah, fondest, blindest, weakest,
> I am He whom thou seekest!

Thompson's poem, which so deeply impressed Chesterton, also influenced Dorothy Day, whose story follows. Other interweaving connections are represented throughout this chapter: C. S. Lewis was influenced by Herbert and Chesterton, and Roger Hughes and Anne Lamott were influenced by Lewis.

The hound of heaven has many agents.

The Possibility of Spiritual Adventure ■ ■
Dorothy Day ■ ■

The climax of Dorothy Day's conversion story is told in the chapter titled "A Child Shall Lead Them." But Dorothy was acquainted with the Hound of Heaven long before her daughter's birth finally brought her to the God she had both longed for and avoided.

Day's family was not religious, but she recalled reading the Bible in her room as a little girl and having a sense of the holy. As a child, she was always drawn to friends and families that were Christian.

A friend named Mary once told her the life story of a saint. Looking back on it, Day couldn't remember the name of the saint, but she recalled the impact the story had on her—the love and gratitude she felt in her heart. She remembered having, "a thrilling recognition of the possibilities of spiritual adventure."[29]

Going to another friend's house to play, Dorothy saw the mother down on her knees praying. Watching the woman pray, Dorothy's heart was flooded with a love and warmth that left a deep impression. And Dorothy emulated the woman for a period of time, praying on her knees.

But while attending university, Day became disenchanted with Christianity and was influenced by political radicals. Marx's slogan "Workers of the world unite. You have nothing to lose but your chains," was the text that thrilled her now.

Not that the longing for God ever went away entirely. Even as a young journalist in New York, hanging out every night in bars and having political discussions with her radical friends, there were reminders. It was on one of those evenings in an atmosphere of smoke and drink, that she first heard "The Hound of Heaven" recited by one of her friends, playwright Eugene O'Neill.

O'Neill had the Francis Thompson poem memorized and would recite it, "black and dour, his head sunk low as he intoned, 'And now my heart is as a broken fount, wherein tear drippings stagnate.'"[30]

Even during this stage when she publicly disowned any faith, Day felt a need to worship. Often after sitting up all night in a bar, she would stop at a church on her way home and kneel in the back. And when she heard O'Neill recite the poem, the idea of the Hound of Heaven fascinated Day.

As she later wrote, "The inevitableness of its outcome made me feel that sooner or later I would have to pause in the mad rush of living and remember my first beginning and my last end."

He Was Talking to Me
Roger Hughes

Roger Hughes grew up with no discernible religious background. When he thought about religion, particularly Christianity, he came to the conclusion that he was an atheist—and he became a rabid one. He always looked for opportunities to denigrate Christianity and organized religion.

One summer when he was in college, he went to Alaska and worked picking salmon out of fishnets. The family he worked for were devout Nazarenes with four daughters (which prompted Roger to hang around more than he otherwise might have).

But he was also drawn to the parents, Wendell and Joyce Honea. They were late converts to Christianity themselves, and Roger was impressed at how welcoming they were; they didn't judge or demean him for not accepting their beliefs. Roger got into discussions with them, but it wasn't possible for him to be strident because of the nature of their lives and their unconditional acceptance of him.

When it was time to return to college, Roger visited the Honeas at their home on Whidbey Island where they lived most of the year. And on Sunday he went to church with them. That's where he had his first real confrontation with a living God. The sermon that Sunday, titled "The Fool," was about different characters of the Bible who were antagonistic to God and how foolish their behavior was. Roger had always seen Christians as the fools, and the sermon turned his worldview on its head. He felt that the sermon was directed at him personally.

He says, "I felt, right to the inner part of me, that the pastor was talking to me. Then he gave an altar call. There was this huge part of me that was yearning to go forward, and I literally gripped the pew with my hands until my knuckles were white to resist going up.

"After the service was over, I decided to talk to the pastor. In an offhanded way, I said 'I'm visiting here and enjoyed your service. I felt that you were talking to me.' And he said. 'Well, I wondered who it was, because that's not the sermon I had prepared for today. I was on my knees last night praying and God gave me this sermon, so I wondered who it was for.'

"I said, 'Thank you very much' and left. I was stunned by what he'd said to me. And then the Honeas told me that that was the first altar call they'd ever heard at that church, which stunned me even more. You would think that all this would be enough to turn someone around. Well, it didn't turn me around, but it brought me up short. It was still just too big a leap for me, intellectually, to accept the concept of a God taking on human flesh."

After going to law school and getting married, Roger decided that his family should find a church. There was something about the church experience that was comforting to him. They moved to a suburban community and started attending an Episcopal church. Roger soon found himself deeply involved in church activities, but still was not a Christian himself.

He believes that his training as a trial lawyer is what made the commitment to Christianity such a hurdle. "As a trial lawyer you tend to be very skeptical. You take nothing at face value, and you don't take anybody's word—you push, you challenge, you explore, you look at every issue from six sides, trying to find the flaw. That's the first characteristic of a good trial attorney.

"And the second thing is, trial attorneys are very slow to come to judgment. One of the biggest mistakes you can make is to come to a conclusion too quickly, before all the facts are in. And so, unknowingly, I exhibited those characteristics in confronting the ultimate question as to whether I could really have a personal relationship with God."

At one point the rector gave a sermon about being a child of God and what that means. Roger remembers that he had "this longing, just a longing in my heart, and a sadness because of a realization that I did not have the relationship that he was talking about."

Then Roger went to a church-sponsored "Faith Alive" weekend retreat. At one point the man leading the retreat invited everyone to get on their knees and follow him in the litany of faith. Roger decided he was not going to miss another chance, and he got on his knees.

As Roger said the words of the litany, he had another remarkable experience: "I had a vision of the layers of my soul being peeled away, like an onion. Layer after layer after layer, peeling away. And I was aware that my whole emotional and intellectual facade was unraveling, until it was smaller and smaller. It was down to the size of a pea, and I recognized that little kernel that was left as the soul of an unbeliever. That's what shocked me, when I saw my innermost being.

"I prayed, 'Please, God, help me with my unbelief,' and felt an overwhelming sense of peace and the sense that God would help me." He continues, "I cannot pinpoint the day and time when I said 'Yes, I do believe,' but at some point I became aware that I absolutely did believe."

Then Roger developed a deep thirst for the Bible and read it intensively. He also read C. S. Lewis's *Mere Christianity* and Josh McDowell's book *Evidence That Demands a Verdict* and found them very persuasive.

Reflecting on his experience, Roger says, "The way I came to faith has made me much more tolerant and less judgmental. I have a real appreciation for how close a call it was for me. I know that my salvation was an act of God's grace and nothing that I did myself. So I have a real heart for those who are struggling."

■ ■ Jesus Would Not Leave
■ ■ *Anne Lamott*

Novelist Anne Lamott had always believed in God. She prayed and had a relationship with God and read books on spirituality. But she didn't believe in Jesus. She says, "I could not for the life of me get that to compute."

At that time she was living in Sausalito, California but was going to a flea market in Marin City on weekends. She loved flea-market food when she was hungover, and she was "often hungover."

While she was at the flea market, she could hear singing coming from a little church down the street and was drawn by the music. So she started going to this African-American Presbyterian church, sitting in the back row and avoiding people. She always left before the sermon because she didn't want to hear the Jesus part. She liked the music, the people, and the sense of community and activism.

After going to this church for a while, Anne started having the feeling that Jesus might be after her. She hadn't been concerned about the possibility of a conversion experience because, from her perspective, there was no reason to have one.

Then Anne became pregnant and had an abortion. When she got home from having the abortion, she began hemorrhaging heavily. She had been drinking but sobered up instantly when she realized that she was in trouble. Instead of calling anyone for help, she tried to clean herself up and take care of everything herself.

But she had a sense that something very bad was happening to her, both physically and spiritually—that her life was on a downward spiral.

This is how Anne describes what happened next: "At about three in the morning, I felt Jesus come into the loft of the houseboat where I had been living for a few years. Through the years, I had always felt my father come into the room if I was in real trouble. But this time I felt Jesus there.

"I thought, 'You have got to be kidding.' Then he took a

seat, kind of cross-legged, sort of Indian-like, at one corner of the houseboat, and I turned to the wall and said out loud, 'I would rather die.' And I really meant it. All of my friends were left-wing, mostly atheists, and Jesus would not leave. It was really awful."

After that, Anne felt very confused and upset. When she attended the little church in Marin City, she still left before the sermons. Yet she continued to have the feeling that she was being pursued.

As to the moment of her conversion, Anne says, "The moment of my conversion was actually a moment of resignation. I was just so exhausted. I had tried to avoid it and then I felt as though, 'OK, I'll open the door,' which is the classic imagery. 'Behold, I stand at the door and knock.'

"So I opened the door and just said, 'What?' I felt as if I had put out food and water, and of course, ironically, I was being given food and water. From then on I started staying through the sermons, but I was still drinking."

The people at her church gave Anne the room she needed, and slowly she got more involved. Eventually she stopped drinking. She says, "All of a sudden I got that voracious hunger you get when you're a baby Christian. Then C. S. Lewis started making a lot of sense to me. But it was still really humiliating to me as an intellectual to be having this experience."

About six months after she got sober, Anne was baptized. The song that was played at her baptism was "There is a balm in Gilead, that makes the wounded whole." Anne hadn't chosen the song, but it felt like ultimate truth to her.

The Most Reluctant Convert in England ■ ■
C. S. Lewis ■ ■

C. S. Lewis, who was to become one of the greatest Christian apologists of the twentieth century, experienced two conversions, both of them reluctant.

The first was from agnosticism to theism. Whatever sense of faith Lewis had acquired in Belfast as a young boy was lost at an English boarding school. A matron at the school, who was exploring theosophy, Rosicrucianism, and spiritualism, had a strong influence on Lewis.

At that time, Lewis's understanding of Christianity was fairly vague, and his teacher's enthusiasms undermined the Christian creed he was familiar with. Her ideas thrilled Lewis, and this introduction left him with a taste for the occult. Lewis later said that it was a "spiritual lust," similar to physical lust in its obsessive nature.

Then Lewis became infatuated with what he called "Northernness"—an intense obsession with the Northern myths of Asgard, the Valkyries, and others. The Norse gods inspired a sense of awe in Lewis that his own religion hadn't. And it had the advantage of not requiring real belief or imposing duties. Lewis had, above all, a desire to be left alone; he intensely disliked interference. The Nordic myths were inspiring but made no demands.

Lewis was a great reader and found himself admiring the work of two Christian writers who were to have a great influence on him: George MacDonald, a Scottish clergyman who wrote Christian fantasies, and G. K. Chesterton, the great Christian apologist. While Lewis didn't agree with the things Chesterton argued for, he couldn't help but admire the quality of his mind. "A young man who wishes to remain a sound atheist cannot be too careful of his reading," he wrote later.

Studying English literature at Oxford, Lewis grew to realize, with some discomfort, that his favorite writers (which now included Johnson, Spenser, Milton, Donne, and Herbert) were all Christians.

"Fine nets and stratagems" were closing in on the scholar. Lewis considered a student named Neville Coghill the most intelligent man in his class and was shocked to learn that Coghill was a Christian. Then one of the most strident atheists he knew remarked that there was good evidence for the historical validity of the Gospels. To top it off, Lewis read, and was deeply impressed by, Chesterton's *Everlasting Man*.

Despite the mounting forays into his intellectual resistance, Lewis held tight to his desire to be left alone. But each night, alone in his room, he felt "the steady unrelenting approach" of the God he wanted to avoid. During that time he dashed off a note to his friend Owen Barfield: "Terrible things are happening to me. The 'Spirit' or 'Real I' is showing an alarming tendency to become much more personal and is taking the offensive, and behaving just like God. You'd better come on Monday at the latest or I may have entered a monastery."[31]

When Lewis finally gave in and admitted that "God was God," he describes himself as, "The most dejected and reluctant convert in all England." At this point Lewis had become a theist but was not yet a Christian. That was another struggle.

Eventually, as a man who had immersed himself in mythology for many years, it became clear to Lewis that Christianity was not a myth. Lewis was especially influenced by a conversation with his friend J. R. R. Tolkien, who believed that in the gospel story mythology is fulfilled. Lewis was persuaded and concluded, "Here and here only in all time the myth must have become fact; the Word, flesh; God, Man."[32]

And finally, Lewis describes a drive to Whipsnade with his brother Warren and says simply, "When we set out I did not believe that Jesus Christ is the Son of God, and when we reached the zoo I did."

■　　　■　　　■

The people in this chapter weren't looking for Jesus, so his entrance into their lives was surprising, even alarming—though ultimately welcome.

Those who knew him during his earthly ministry were also surprised by Jesus, by what he said and did. His answers to questions were often completely unexpected.

Once the disciples asked him who would be the greatest in the kingdom of heaven. Jesus called a little child over and said that unless the disciples became like a little child they would never enter the kingdom of heaven. (Meaning, possibly, that they should be less concerned about status.) Then he said: "Take care that you do not despise one of these little ones; for, I tell you, in heaven their angels continually see the face of my Father in heaven" (Matthew 18:10–11).

Jesus went on to say, "What do you think? If a shepherd has a hundred sheep, and one of them has gone astray, does he not leave the ninety-nine on the mountains and go in search of the one that went astray? And if he finds it, truly I tell you, he rejoices over it more than over the ninety-nine that never went astray. So it is not the will of your Father in heaven that one of these little ones should be lost" (Matthew 18:12–14).

The hound of heaven and the good shepherd are metaphors that teach us the same thing: To God, everyone matters.

CHAPTER TEN

Signs and Wonders

The world is charged with the grandeur of God.
It will flame out, like shining from shook foil.

—Gerard Manley Hopkins

At times, God reveals himself in miraculous ways—in signs and wonders—as we read in so many Old and New Testament stories. And God is still at work in the world today, revealing himself in many ways.

Some people actually hear God's voice or have visions. The men and women who told me about miraculous interventions, in this chapter and others, were generally not looking for them. People who've had these experiences are sometimes reluctant to discuss them. These things aren't supposed to happen, and people may think you're crazy if you talk about them.

There may be other reasons that people react negatively to these stories—one of them is envy. Those of us who've never received a vision or visitation may feel a little jealous of this special attention from God. I personally have never had visions or heard a voice, though I have had an epiphany and once was sure that God was laughing at me.

Another reaction is fear. If God were to speak to me, would I be ready to listen? Frederick Buechner writes: "God's coming is always unforeseen, I think, and the reason, if I had to guess, is that if he gave us anything much in the way of advance warning, more often than not we would have made ourselves scarce long before he got there."[33] The encounters with God related in this chapter were all unforeseen—but gratefully received.

■ ■ The Presence of Love
■ ■ *Simone Weil*

The French writer Simone Weil was a philosopher and an activist. She taught for a while but lost her position because of her support for striking workers. During the Spanish Civil

War, she trained with an Anarchist unit, but returned home after being injured in a cooking accident. Later, Simone and her family, who were Jewish (but not religious) were able to leave France and escape to the United States, safe from the Nazis during World War II. But Simone insisted on returning to England to work for the resistance, eating only what the official French ration allowed.

While she was involved in this political activity, she was also going through a conversion process. As an intellectual, Simone had read widely but had never had any interest in mystical works. So it came as a complete surprise to her when she had a mystical experience. She was reading George Herbert's "Love bade me welcome while my Soul drew back," a poem she often recited because of its beautiful language, but at some point the lines became a prayer.

"Christ came down and took possession of me," she later wrote. "In my arguments about the insolubility of the problem of God I had never foreseen the possibility of that, of a real contact, person to person, here below, between a human being and God. I had vaguely heard tell of things of this kind, but I had never believed in them. . . . In this sudden possession of me by Christ, neither my senses nor my imagination had any part; I only felt in the midst of my suffering the presence of a love like that which one can read in the smile on a beloved face."[34]

Hearing God's Voice ■ ■
Saint Augustine ■ ■

Augustine was born in Northern Africa in the year 354 to a Christian mother and a pagan father (who became a Christian convert late in life). An incredibly bright and talented scholar, Augustine was put off by Christian texts, which he found crudely translated.

He became involved in Manichaeism, a religion that espoused a total duality between good and evil and taught that we aren't responsible for the evil we do because we do it under the control of the evil destroyer. This was a comforting doctrine to Augustine, who had indulged in a number of youthful vices. He had many questions about Manichaeism, however, and was told that they would all be answered by Faustus, the leader of the sect. When Faustus finally came to town, Augustine was completely disappointed with the man and the answers he gave.

As an ambitious young scholar, Augustine grew restless in the provinces of the empire and moved to Milan, where he became the professor of rhetoric for the imperial court. Augustine had lived with a woman for many years and had a child with her without marrying her. He now abandoned her to become engaged to a more suitable society wife, and while he was waiting for his fiancée to come of age he took another mistress.

In the meantime, Augustine's mother had moved to Rome and had gotten to know Ambrose, the venerable Bishop of Milan. Under Ambrose's influence, Augustine was drawn to the truth of Christianity. But he found himself in moral conflict. Augustine later wrote that he was convicted of the truth but kept answering God, "Presently, leave me but a little." And he confessed that "presently, presently had no present and my little while went on for a long while."[35]

At one point, Augustine went to the country with a group of friends and found himself pacing in the garden, wrestling with his feelings of guilt. Then he heard a voice saying, "Take up and read. Take up and read." At first he thought the it was a child's voice and wondered whether there were children playing some game nearby. Then he realized that God was telling him to pick up the Bible and read it. When he did pick it up, the book opened to Romans 13:13, where he read the passage, "Let us walk honestly as in the day, not in rioting and drunkenness; not in promiscuity and debauchery, not in quarreling and envying."

Augustine took this as a direct command from God concerning his life: "For instantly, as the sentence ended, there was infused in my heart something like light of full certainty and all the gloom of doubt vanished away."

Augustine eventually became the Bishop of Hippo and one of the most influential Christian theologians in the history of the church.

A Vision ■ ■
Mark Simon ■ ■

Mark Simon was a folksinger who performed in concerts around the country for years. But he became disillusioned with the music world and in doing so went through a major life crisis.

In the middle of that crisis, Mark recalls, "I was lifted up out of that morass of confusion and given a gracious gift. Out of my sense of my shortcomings and my own inability to break through a circle of things I was involved in, there came a crystal clear vision of a potential I had which was much greater than the confines of my activities and my feelings about myself."

The experience felt like a tremendous natural high. For months Mark felt a new ability to communicate and to do anything or be anything that he wanted. In one particular contemplative session he imagined himself climbing up a ladder of all the things he could become. At the top of that ladder a consciousness of God began to dawn on him.

"That was the first I'd really thought about God in my life," Mark remembers. "The thought came to me that all these things I worried about didn't matter much, that it was more important to be what God wanted me to be than to achieve any particular worldly success."

After a few months the euphoric state of revelation left him, and he found himself in a state of limbo or suspended animation. He couldn't go back to the way he had been, but he no longer had the sense of grace from the vision.

Reflecting on that time, Mark says, "I wanted to find out what had happened to me in that experience and I wanted to recapture the feeling of grace, so I went through a search that led me through a lot of cultic and universalist teachings. But the Lord had his hand on me and led me through and out of that search to himself and to a church that acknowledged Jesus. It was the beginning of a path that led me back to that freedom that I'd had a glimpse of. It gave me something to hold on to."

At one point Mark was in a church service where he accepted Jesus as his Lord and Savior. Mark feels that the decision was not wholehearted, that at the time he was merely acknowledging Christianity as part of his spiritual search. But he says, "When I made that commitment, the Lord honored it. And the name of Jesus came alive in my life, and I was led toward things that were Christian."

Although Mark's family background was Jewish, he says it didn't cause him any conflict. Instead it led him to a greater understanding of the continuity between the Old and New Testaments. He saw that "Jesus is prophesied as being the Messiah in so many passages in the Old Testament, I'm delighted in seeing myself as a completed Jew."

After Mark came through his life crisis, he went back to his first love, painting. His new series of landscapes were a phenomenal success. Since then, Mark says, the Lord has given him a new vision as an artist. One series combines his love of art and music—expressionist calligraphy dropped on paper with an ink dropper. He says, "In some ways it denotes praising God. It's an expression of joy."

A Dream ■ ■
Mary Poplin ■ ■

Mary Poplin was raised in a nominal Christian home where she learned some Bible stories in Sunday school. But she never really connected with the church and, as an adult, she drifted away. Eventually she went to graduate school and became a professor. During the early years of her academic career, she was interested in every new philosophy, and she explored a variety of religions and spiritualities.

In 1991 she was doing research in inner-city schools and met some children who should have been in trouble but were doing fine. They turned out to be Christians. Mary just thought they were weird. At the time, she also had a friend who persistently said two things to her. One was: "If you would ever like help with your spiritual life, I would like to help you." And the other was: "Do you believe in evil?" As it turns out, Mary says, "He was praying for me for about eight years. He was really interceding for me."

After the research project was done, Mary had a disturbing dream. "I was in a long line of people, and I couldn't see the beginning of the line or the end of the line. It was so long, it looked like it went on forever. We were all in gray robes, and people were passing something on the way. When I finally got to that point, I saw that it was like Leonardo da Vinci's painting of the Last Supper and it was in color. The disciples were sitting, looking out, like they were in the painting. But Christ was not at the table with them; he was standing and greeting us in the line. When I saw him I felt so ashamed that I fell down at his feet and started crying. I couldn't even look at him, but he touched my shoulder. And when I woke up, I was actually physically crying."

Mary remembered her friend's offer to help. She called and told him about her dream and said that she needed to address her spiritual life. They met at a restaurant and over dinner he asked, "Why do you want to do something with your spiritual life now?" And Mary heard herself say that she sensed that there was something dark in her heart. Her friend listened and then said, "Well, since Christ is in your dream, maybe you'd like to start reading the New Testament." Mary hadn't known that he was a Christian. He was part Native American, and she had assumed that he was into some kind of Native-American spirituality. But she knew that he lived his life differently than anyone else.

Several months later, Mary's mother wanted to visit her childhood home in a town in North Carolina, and Mary accompanied her. They went to a little church and sat in the back. Mary doesn't remember anything the minister said except one statement right before communion. "You don't have to be a member of this or any church to take communion here," he said. "But you do have to believe that Jesus Christ lived and died for your sins, and you have to want him in your life." Mary had been reading the Bible for a couple of months by the time she heard that invitation to communion. She said, "Something came over me. I thought, 'Even if a tornado rips through this building, I'm going to get to that communion table.' I did get there. And I remember kneeling down and praying, 'Please come and get me, please come and get me.'"

Mary had a sabbatical coming up. During that time she met Christians from many different churches, and the one thing they all had in common was the Bible. She developed an insatiable desire for reading Scripture. She read it over and over, listened to it on tape, and went to Christian conferences. At a monastery in New Mexico, she was taking notes and realized that when she wrote Scripture down, she saw things that she hadn't seen before. So for the next eight months, she copied the New Testament, Psalms, and Proverbs by hand. In retrospect she thinks that the immersion in Scripture was healing her mind, because she had been so deeply into the philosophies of the world.

Mary wants to work with other Christians across denominational lines and across ethnic lines. She says, "Even though I'm of European extraction, of all the people who've taught me what it means to be a Christian, not one has been Euro-American."

She has seen some of her students come to the Lord and is part of a group of Christian professors and graduate students who meet and encourage each other. Mary says, "God has given me a vision that he wants a place in his universities. Working toward that end has become part of my calling."

■ ■ The Panther
■ ■ *Amy Sullivan*

Two years ago, Amy Sullivan had reached a point in her life when she "opened up into grief—grief that had been in my own life, and that had probably been generationally passed down. I was going through a three-year dark night of the soul and had to walk back through all the traumas of my childhood. It was terrible."

Amy had been raised in a church where God was an idea but was never talked about in a personal way. She had no prayer life or any sense that she needed God. But she was in such pain that for the first time in her adult life, she began asking God for help. And she received it. It was on a hike through the Santa Cruz mountains in California. She was all by herself and feeling very alone and very scared. She said "Jesus, please be with me and help me. I am so frightened."

And, she remembers, in that moment he came: "It's hard to describe how—it was in the form of a vision. He works with each of us very differently. It was the presence of God, and I had no conception of what to do with it. I knew it wasn't me, but I didn't say it was God."

Then Amy started attending a Presbyterian church and joined the Stephen's Ministry (a group of caregivers). She says, "Week after week, the Lord's love was reflected in the eyes of the other people in the course." Amy also went to the church's pastor and told him about her mystical experience in the Santa Cruz mountains. He told her, "God is definitely working in your life." Looking back on that time she is grateful that the pastor didn't discount her experience. He also shared the Gospel with her several times. But Amy wasn't ready to hear it.

She says, "It didn't really get through to me that it was all about Jesus. I was so resistant. Then he started to hound me. Sometimes I would feel this presence, like a panther, a black panther, watching me and following me. It was definitely something good and definitely something persistent. I literally felt followed by Christ. I would see him behind a door, with his sandaled feet. But he wouldn't open the door; he was waiting for me to open the door. Finally one night, in the middle of a Neil Young concert, I said, "I can't take another step forward. OK, Christ, I guess you can come in."

After having these visions, Amy wondered for a while whether she was crazy. Then she read Anne Lamott's book *Traveling Mercies,* and discovered that something very similar had happened to the writer, so maybe she wasn't so crazy. Yet despite the visions, Amy's life hadn't changed. She still felt terrible.

One day Amy had a very difficult conversation with her husband and, for a short period of time, she lost her daughter in a department store. That night she experienced the deepest despair of her life.

She remembers: "I woke up in the middle of the night, and Jesus was there. I said, 'Oh, it's you.' And he said, 'It is I.' And I said, 'I love you,' And he said, 'I know. I love you too.' And I realized that I had a choice to make—whether or not to give him my heart. I did give him my heart; and he gave it back to me. I gave him my life and he gave it back to me, and what I was given back was a different life.

"The next morning when I woke up, I could hear the angels singing. I knew inside that what I was hearing were angels. But when you try to put words to an experience like that, it so diminishes it.

"God has set everything right between him and me. Scripture reassures us that no one who trusts God with heart and soul will ever regret it. It's the same for all of us; God will act in the same incredibly generous way to anyone who calls out to him for help."

■   ■   ■

The people in this chapter all had extraordinary encounters with God. But any rebirth or reconnection with God is a supernatural event—a change of heart and life. God's ongoing work of redemption in our lives is also miraculous.

In this chapter's introduction I mentioned a personal epiphany. This is what happened. Driving onto the Bay Bridge that connects Berkeley with San Francisco, I faced long lines of clogged traffic, a dreaded sight. All of a sudden I was overwhelmed with an impression of how God saw this same congested bridge. I experienced an enormous love and compassion for the people in all those cars. It was an incredible feeling that came from outside myself and lasted only a few seconds.

What I felt was completely different from my normal attitude toward fellow drivers (believe me). It was a rare glimpse into what seemed like a parallel universe, a realm of love. It was an experience that I'll always value. Yet God's day-to-day presence in my life, his abiding, unchanging love, is even more miraculous than that epiphany.

CHAPTER ELEVEN

The Character of God

Nature is God's great revelation of himself,
his richness, his complexity,
his intelligence, his beauty, his mystery,
his great power and glory.
The hints and clues to his nature
are everywhere.

—Luci Shaw

God reveals himself to us in a variety of ways, including through his creation. Romans 1:20 tells us: "Ever since the creation of the world his eternal power and divine nature, invisible though they are, have been understood and seen through the things he has made." Psalm 19:1 tells us: "The heavens declare the glory of God, the vault of heaven proclaims his handiwork."

Since the creation of Adam and Eve, God has been in relationship with human beings. But even the people of Israel, God's covenant people, were awed by God's holiness. After receiving the Ten Commandments, Moses' face shown so brightly from being in God's presence that people were afraid to come near him.

When God appeared to Moses in a burning bush and Moses asked who he was, God answered: "I am that I am." Centuries later in a conversation with followers, Jesus said, "before Abraham was, I am" (John 8:58). Jesus deliberately used these words to let the Jews know that he was the promised Messiah. Christians believe that this claim is true—that Jesus is the son of God.

Jesus is the way God chose to reveal himself to us. He became the human face of God. Looking at Jesus' life, we get insight into God's character—his love, mercy, and forgiveness. We see God's humility in being born as a tiny, helpless, human infant. We see the compassion that Jesus showed toward those who were physically sick and spiritually empty and understand that he wants us to be made whole. We understand that he cares about the eternal part of us, our souls, and he cares about our daily life here on earth, a life that he chose to share with us.

In this chapter, people who were drawn to faith by something they saw in God's character tell their stories.

The Prodigal ■ ■
Marian Dan ■ ■

Marian grew up in Romania with a Christian mother and an atheist father. As a teenager, he was very wild and rebellious, although his brothers and sister were devout Christians.

Under the communists it was OK to be a Christian as long as you didn't proselytize, which meant no producing or distributing Christian literature, including Bibles. So other European Christians smuggled Bibles in to the Romanians. Marian recalls that the Irish were the best at it. They would go through customs in a motor home with a bunch of kids making noise and the customs officers would say, "Go on. Get out of here." Then they'd drive along a highway and drop the Bibles out of their car without stopping, and Romanian Christians would run out of the woods and pick them up.

Marian's brother was involved in this Bible smuggling so he saw thousands of Bibles at home—many of them destined for the Soviet Union. But after years of living under a totalitarian communist regime that controlled the press and distorted the truth, Marian didn't believe anything that he read and was not interested in the Bibles.

However, growing up in a devout family, Marian had learned a lot about Christianity. He would even argue for the existence of God with his atheist friends. But the temptations of youth were too great, and he didn't want to abandon his carefree lifestyle. He knew that his mother prayed for him every day, and he even asked her to stop. She was very arthritic, but still Marian would find her down on her knees praying.

One Sunday when his family was at church, Marian turned on the radio and heard a Romanian preacher, Joseph Tsan. As he listened to the message, Marian was convicted of his sin. He says, "What really moved me was the love of God. I suddenly realized how much patience the Lord had with me for so many terrible sins. But he didn't take his revenge on me or say, 'That's it, Marian. I'm finished with you.' That's what made me reconsider. The combination of conviction for my sins and God's love led to my repentance. I promised God I'd do better, and of course I failed many times, but that message was the turning point in my life.

"In a way I was like the prodigal son. I knew the father's house yet rebelled in willful disobedience. But still he welcomed me back."

■ ■ Our Great Advocate
■ ■ *Adam Huston*

Adam Huston was raised in a church-going family, but he stopped attending after college. He got a business degree to please his father, but then followed his own interests by going to art school and studying photography. While in art school in the 1960s, he went through a few years of sowing wild oats. He didn't have any mentors or models spiritually during that period and was very focused on producing his artwork. Eventually he moved to Copenhagen to teach photography and, while there, he met the woman he would marry. God was just not something he was thinking about.

When Adam came back to the United States and moved

to Mendocino with his bride, he started going to church again. At church he met David, who had retired to Mendocino. They became friends, and David would talk about things that were important to him—Christian books he was reading and classes that he was taking. Adam was impressed. He thought, "David seems to have it together. His values are pretty right on, and he's a happy guy. He's satisfied with his life."

After going to church for a while, Adam wanted to learn more about the Bible but didn't think he could study it on his own by just sitting down and reading it. Then a friend asked whether Adam would like to be part of a Bible study they were starting. Adam says, "I was primed. I was ready." The Bible study became a regular part of his life. One thing Adam had learned from photography was that if you really want to learn something, try teaching it. Taking his turn leading the study turned into a major growth experience for Adam who says, "I'd get commentaries out and spend days studying the passage."

If someone asked Adam when he became a born-again Christian, he says he couldn't give an exact year. But every once in a while when he was preparing at Bible study, a word would really speak to him.

In an earlier part of his life, Adam had been attracted to some New Age ideas like astrology and reincarnation. As a new Christian, he was trying to reconcile Christianity and reincarnation. He wrote a paper on it for a New College Berkeley class and showed it to the professor, Bill Dyrness, who told him it was off base and said, "You really need to take another look at this." So Adam put it away, but the issue wasn't really resolved in his mind.

Then, when Adam was studying the Bible, a word jumped out at him in a way that seemed supernatural. The word was "futile," and it was in a passage in Romans. Adam says, "What I understood God to be saying at that point was, 'You're asking the wrong question. The question of whether reincarnation is true or not is a futile question. You're putting your energy in the wrong direction.'" He looked up the definition of "futile" and it said, "having no benefit." He realized that he should have been asking, "'What should I be focusing on?' Somewhere along the line I understood that if you focus on God, he will reveal the truth that is important for you to have."

Adam sees his conversion as a series of stairsteps. David's mentoring was the first step. The Bible study was the second step. The studies at New College were the third. The fourth was the revelation he had with the verse in Romans. Then there was a fifth step (which he is in now) when he studied at a YWAM (Youth with a Mission) training center.

The YWAM teaching focused on the character of God. Adam says, "I learned that there is no greater advocate for us than Jesus Christ. When we fall he picks us up and puts us back on the path. I learned about the loving gracious character of God, that I no longer need to cringe in God's presence, that I was accepted. I had the idea that following God's will was kind of like taking medicine—good for you but hard to take. But God is like the perfect father who wants the best for his children. He really wants to bless us."

Adam is now in the Ukraine with YWAM, leading Bible studies with university students.

The Beginning of Eternal Life ■ ■
Thomas Merton ■ ■

Thomas Merton was born in France, on the border of Spain, in January 1915. Both his parents were artists. After his mother's death, his father traveled around the world, at times taking Thomas with him and at times leaving him with relatives.

Thomas lived an unsettled life. For a while he stayed in New York with his grandparents, whom he describes as Protestants who never went to church. He lived in Bermuda, went back to France, and then went to school in England. He attended Clare College, Cambridge, briefly, but lost his scholarship as a result of his "riotous living." He then moved back to New York where he ended up earning two degrees at Columbia University. He describes himself during this period as a child of the modern world "tangled up in petty and useless concerns with myself, and almost incapable of even considering or understanding anything that was really important to my own true interests."[36]

He fell in love with a girl who humiliated him, lied to him, and, in short, treated him as badly as he had treated other women. He developed a bleeding ulcer. He also spent time with friends getting drunk and arguing about mysticism.

During this time, Merton met a Hindu monk named Bramachari whose asceticism and critique of American materialism impressed him greatly. It was Bramachari who suggested that Merton should read Augustine's *Confessions* and Thomas à Kempis's *Imitation of Christ*. Merton found himself drawn to the Christian faith, at least at the theoretical level, and decided to write his master's thesis on Francis Blake, the English artist and Christian mystic. In practice, however, he was still "completely charmed and fettered by my worldly attachments."

A young priest gradually convinced Merton that Jesus Christ was more than a good man or a great prophet—that, in fact, he was God incarnate. Listening to a sermon one Sunday, Merton felt that he had been given the grace to believe. In hearing and believing for the first time, he experienced a deep sense of peace. Leaving the church and walking down Broadway, he felt himself to be in a new world. He wanted to be baptized and take communion.

When Merton took his first communion, he experienced a revelation about the character of God. He felt himself enter "God's own gravitation toward the depths of His own infinite nature, His goodness without end. And God that center Who is everywhere, and whose circumference is nowhere, finding me, through incorporation with Christ, incorporated into this immense and tremendous gravitational movement which is love, which is the Holy Spirit, loved me."

Years later, looking back on his conversion experience, Merton said that he was not looking for religion but was seeking the living God.

■ ■ A Reflection of God's Beauty
■ ■ *Krystyna Sanderson*

Krystyna Sanderson was born in Poland and raised as a Roman Catholic. She attended church regularly and looked forward to her first communion, hoping that something marvelous would happen. She thought that God would come to her and that finally she would be happy, that all her problems would go away. She had a beautiful white dress and great expectations. But then the big day arrived—and nothing changed. Krystyna was devastated. She told herself, "Forget it.

I'll just go my own merry way because God doesn't care. He didn't do what I wanted him to do."

Years later, Krystyna moved to Texas where she studied painting and photography. She had always been fascinated by human faces and even more by photographs of human faces. She didn't know who was really behind a face or who was behind each human being. All she knew was that she was drawn to the beauty and mystery of the people she photographed. She started to work on a photographic series, "Masks." She saw the face as a mask that concealed rather than revealed the inner person. People could be smiling and looking happy yet be extremely sad inside. That was Krystyna's own situation. She was profoundly unhappy. "There was something in me that was aching," she recalls. "I couldn't even find the words for it. The series 'Masks' was a visual manifestation that I was in great unrest, searching."

She photographed all kinds of people—African Americans, Native Americans, and Caucasians, old and young. Her work was eventually published in a photographic album called *Masks*.

Later she moved to New York. She says, "I make fun of myself now, but at the time I came to New York to become rich and famous." But being in New York didn't help; she continued to feel lost and unhappy. Then Krystyna met a woman, a Jewish believer, who talked to her about Jesus Christ. For the first time in her life, Krystyna began to see that her emotional recovery and spiritual recovery might go hand in hand.

Krystyna's new Christian friend quoted the verse, "Come to me, all you that are weary and are carrying heavy burdens, and I will give you rest" (Matthew 11:28). Krystyna says, "I'll never forget that. I felt like Christ said these words directly to me—like he was standing there. It was so profound. I had never read the Bible in my life. I felt trapped in my emotions and by the way I was living. And then this voice reached out to me saying, 'I can give you whatever you need to heal your soul and your heart and your life. I have the power and authority to do it.'

"I was given an explanation for why my life didn't work. Because I was not supposed to live on my own. Everything became totally crystal clear. I had a tremendous sense of peace when I realized that I was God's creature."

Looking back, Krystyna realizes that God did come to her—even if it didn't happen in Lodz, on the Sunday that she took her first communion. She says, "I understand now that God doesn't come to us on demand, but he does come if we invite him and want him in our life."

Reflecting on her photographic series "Masks," she says, "I believe now that I was drawn to those faces because they revealed something about the image of God, in which we are all made. There was beauty and mystery in each face I photographed. Those faces were speaking to me, because behind each face hid the Creator. I see my art as a dim reflection of God's goodness and beauty, and I see God as the ultimate Artist."

■　　■　　■

Many people in this book mentioned the brilliant Christian apologist, C. S. Lewis. A confirmed bachelor for many years, Lewis was well into middle age when he met and married an American named Joy Davidman, whom he lost to cancer three years later. Their love story and his subsequent loss are documented in the movie *Shadowlands* and in Lewis's book *A Grief Observed.*

Davidman, who was Jewish by birth, had been an ardent communist before her Christian conversion, which was greatly influenced by Lewis's writings. She later wrote a wonderful book of reflections on the Ten Commandments called *Smoke on the Mountain.*

In her chapter on the first commandment, "I am the Lord your God . . . you shall have no other gods before me," she talks about the gods of paganism and polytheism and their demands for sacrifice. She concludes: "Then came the knowledge of God. An almost unimaginable person—a single being, creator of heaven and earth, not to be bribed with golden images or children burned alive; loving only righteousness. A being who demanded your whole heart."[37]

CHAPTER TWELVE

Other Voices

*Something irreplaceable is lost if your kinds
of loving, your ways of serving God, are missing.
Each of you is an incredible occurrence.*

—Bishop Desmond Tutu

To Americans, Christianity may seem like a European religion, but that is not the case. Art historian Laurel Gasque writes: "Historically Christianity has united with its locale and spoken its argot. So much so that it has often been considered a European or western religion, forgetting its origins at the confluence of Asia and Africa. The past, however, is not truly necessary to remind us of that—if we open our eyes to what is currently occurring. If we look today at the dispersion of Christianity in the world, we see that Christianity has migrated. Its heartland is no longer Europe or the West, but it is moving into Africa and Asia. It is reinventing itself in Latin America and Eurasia (the former U.S.S.R.)."[38]

This chapter relates the conversion stories of non-westerners, two of whom were former Hindus—Asian Indians who came to faith in the west. But one of the oldest Christian communities in the world is in southern India, where the church traces its roots back to a missionary trip by Thomas, the first century Apostle.

Several years ago, on a flight to Los Angeles, I was seated next to an Asian man who was wearing a suit and reading an Asian text. I decided he was a businessman and went on with my own reading. As we neared LAX, I had the strong sense that the man was praying over the text, and eventually asked him what he was reading. He told me it was the Bible. Then he said that he was a Christian clergyman from Korea going to Los Angeles as a missionary. Although I was intrigued by this, I wasn't completely surprised. Seoul, Korea, has some of the largest Christian churches in the world. At least ten of them have ten thousand or more members and almost round-the-clock services. One Korean mega-church has nearly a quarter million members.

The pastor on that plane to Los Angeles wasn't the first non-western missionary I'd met. When I was a child growing up in Los Angeles, my parents were deeply influenced by some African ministers who had been part of the great East African Revival. Many Christians went to their conferences in Southern California to learn how to walk closer with God.

More recently, in my work with *Radix* magazine, I met and interviewed Alex Mukulu, a missionary from Africa, who was touring with a singing and drumming group. His conversion story follows.

The Prince of Peace
Alex Mukulu

Alex Mukulu is a Ugandan actor, musician, and director, and the former National Educational Secretary of Uganda's Cultural Association. When Alex first started writing and directing, he formed a drama troupe called The African Social and International Theater of the Absurd. This was in 1977 during the brutal military regime of Idi Amin. It was a difficult time to live through or have much hope, and Alex found life meaningless—everything seemed absurd.

Then Alex began working on a play called "The Prince of Peace." He says, "In our country there was no peace at all. We were fighting for twenty years. I wanted to create a character who could be a symbol of peace and a model for as many people as we could reach with this particular play."

Alex often walked by a house where a man sat by a window reading. He grew curious about the man and stopped one day to ask what he was reading. Alex introduced himself as a playwright and said that he was working on a play called

"The Prince of Peace." The man said that he was reading the Bible, and that he had read the Bible twice every year for fifty years. The fact that the man had read this book so often was something that Alex couldn't understand.

Then the man said to Alex, "You cannot give what you don't have. If you want to give people peace, you need to have peace. The peace you need is the peace of Jesus Christ." Then he said, "If you want this peace, I will pray for you." So Alex knelt down, prayed, and became a Christian.

When I met him in San Francisco, Alex told me he was a missionary to the United States. He explained, "I'm talking about the same Christ. But God made the world in diversity—and at times someone from a different culture can explain the same thing, and people understand it better than they would if it had been explained to them by their own people."

■ ■ More Than a Religion
■ ■ *Xiao Li Wong*

When Xiao Li was growing up in China, he was taught about the evils of religion. Xiao Li grew up to be a scholar, and in his intellectual circles there were many discussions about the crisis of spirit in China since the Cultural Revolution. Xiao Li and his friends began to think that Christianity could be good for Chinese society, which they felt had become too materialistic.

When Xiao Li came to the United States as a visiting scholar, he met a pastor at a local church, and as they talked, Xiao Li became more and more interested in Christianity. Through these conversations he came to believe in a God who created the universe. But he had no thoughts about a relationship with Christ. He says, "I came to the church to investigate

Christianity, thinking that it might be a good ideology for China. As an atheist I certainly had no expectations about personally encountering God."

Then he began attending an Alpha class, a practical introduction to the Christian faith. He found the classes well-organized and the discussions helpful. Bit by bit he began believing and started reading the Bible every night. He was especially moved by the New Testament passages about love—God's love for us, our love for God, and our love for each other.

Xiao Li had a growing passion to accept God. But he thought he wasn't ready, that he needed to change first before becoming a Christian. Then he read several books that helped him realize that after you become a Christian, your life changes over time, by faith and love. So he decided to take the first step and leave the rest to God. He says, "There is a difference in my mind and heart. After I prayed I felt more peaceful. The way I view other people has changed; they seem more accepting and kinder than I used to think."

Before he came to the United States, Xiao Li knew nothing about the church in China. Now he knows about the house-church movement. As a member of the communist party, Christian conversion is a sensitive issue for Xiao Li. He says, "When I return, I will be able to talk about my faith to my friends, but not to my colleagues."

Reading *More Than a Carpenter,* by Josh McDowell, helped Xiao Li believe that Jesus is the Son of God. Something at the end of that book meant a lot to him. He says, "I learned that Christianity is not a religion. Religion is about people trying to find God through their own hard work. Christianity is God coming and knocking on your door and loving you."

■ ■ A New Program
■ ■ *Kumar Subramanian*

Kumar was raised in a Hindu home in India. His family worshiped many gods and followed several gurus. He was bothered by the way he was treated "like a little prince" compared to his sisters who were given lesser educational opportunities. He was also bothered by how badly workers were treated in the first company he worked for. He says, "India is a highly structured society based on the caste system. People receive status based on their profession; if you are a farmer or a fisherman you are at the bottom of the list."

When Kumar decided to go to the United States to study the computer industry, he chose a school that was headed by one of the most respected Asian Indians in North America. This man was admired both for his brilliance in the technology field and his knowledge of Hindu culture and scripture.

But from the first day he arrived at the school, Kumar was deeply disappointed in the man's character. He says, "I could not even imagine an illiterate person doing the kinds of things that he was doing. I had put him on a pedestal, and now as I watched his behavior I became really depressed."

Kumar was trying to follow the teachings of the Bhagavad Gita, a Hindu scripture, so he went to the professor and confronted him with what Hindu scripture said about his behavior. The man answered, "Who follows these scriptures anymore?" This response completely shattered Kumar. His former admiration of the man turned into hatred. He felt like he was going to die.

Deciding he needed to move on, Kumar sat in his car and prayed—not to any specific Hindu god, but simply to God, saying, "I am willing to take on anything you lead me to, even if it's difficult or dangerous. But I am willing to take the risk if you will show yourself to me."

Kumar drove north and pulled into a gas station about twenty-five miles from Seattle. A woman was standing there, and something made him approach her. He asked her about a cheap place to stay while he was looking for a job. They talked for about five or ten minutes. Then the woman gave Kumar her phone number and said that if he needed help, he should call her.

After he found a place to stay, Kumar called the woman who invited him to her church. Kumar thought, "There are no Hindu temples around here, so why don't I go to a church, since Jesus Christ is one of the gods. So I went to a Presbyterian church for the Sunday evening worship."

In his sermon that night the pastor, Earl Palmer, said that Abraham and Moses were not people to be worshiped. Rather, they are to be looked to for the faith they had in God. Kumar was totally amazed. He'd been expected to worship the Hindu gurus without even looking at their character. He assumed that Biblical heroes like Abraham and Moses were worshiped by Christians.

Kumar went back to the church and in another sermon he heard that John the Baptist expected the Messiah to kill bad people and restore order. Kumar says, "That's exactly what the Hindus believe, that Krishna comes and talks and if people don't listen, he will just wipe them out. I learned that Jesus Christ came to forgive the sins of the people. This really touched me. I prayed, 'God, if what this person is preaching is true, and if you're the one that he's talking about will you reveal yourself to me?'"

In the next sermon, during his concluding remarks, Earl

Palmer said, "Jesus is mellow—really kind, really gentle, really tender." As Kumar listened to those words, something happened to him. It was instantaneous and wonderful, but he didn't know what it was.

Kumar says, "That night when I went home I felt something changing all through my body. Since I'm a software guy I thought, 'Some new program is running inside me.' Something was telling me to get up and read the Bible. And I didn't know what was telling me this or why. When I came out of my room, my roommate said to me, 'Kumar, you look different.' I said, 'Well, I think I'm going to become a Christian.'"

"He said 'What?!' because all during the time I was staying with him, I had been telling him how wonderful Hinduism was and how it even encompassed Christianity. I was also surprised when those words came out of my mouth. Then I realized what was happening; I could feel the Spirit in me."

Since that time Kumar's faith has grown. He has even been able to let go of his hatred toward the professor. Kumar says, "I believe that God has a plan for every person's life. All you need is this tiny mustard seed of faith. If you have that, God will redeem you."

■ ■ The Gift of Salvation
■ ■ *Pandita Ramabai*

Pandita Ramabai was born in 1858 in the Mangalore District of India to a Brahmin family. Her father was a devout Hindu, a well-educated man who was an independent thinker. He was determined that his wife and his children, including his daughters, should be educated. So Ramabai started life as a literate Hindu woman, which was very rare at that time.

Ramabai's father was continually persecuted by their neighbors for educating his daughters and not marrying Ramabai off as a child.

Ramabai's father had been born into wealth, but the lifelong religious pilgrimages he took his family on and the ashram he founded depleted his fortune. After her parents' deaths in the famine of 1876–77, Ramabai joined her older brother on pilgrimages to sacred sites throughout India, undergoing long fasts and other depravations in an effort to become holy.

Over the years, as Ramabai studied Hindu scripture, she found many contradictions. What one text would describe as righteous behavior another would describe as unrighteous. But she found the texts in agreement on one subject—that women, of all castes, were bad, worse than demons.

She wrote: "The only hope of women getting this much-desired liberation from Karma and its results, that is, countless millions of births and deaths and untold suffering, was the worship of their husbands. . . . She is to worship him with whole-hearted devotion as the only god, to know and see no other pleasure in life except in the most degraded slavery to him. The woman has no right to study the Vedas and Vedanta, and without knowing them, no one can know the Brahma. Without knowing Brahma, no one can get liberation; therefore no woman as a woman can get liberation, that is, Moksha."[39]

After her brother died when she was twenty-two, Ramabai married his close friend, an attorney from a lower caste. Although it was forbidden to marry outside her caste, neither Ramabai nor her husband believed in the caste system any longer. After two years of marriage, Ramabai's husband died of cholera, leaving her with a young daughter. Wanting to become better educated, Ramabai used earnings from a book she wrote to finance a trip to England for herself and her daughter.

In England she was taken in by the Sisters of Wantage, who treated her kindly and introduced her to Christian teaching. At one point, the Mother Superior arranged a trip for Pandita to visit a home the Sisters ran in London for former prostitutes, many of whom had completely changed their lives as a result of the gospel and the care of the Sisters. This visit had an enormous impact on Ramabai.

She said, "Here for the first time in my life I came to know that something should be done to reclaim the so-called fallen women. . . . I had never heard or seen anything done for this class of women by the Hindus in my own country. The law of the Hindu commands that the king shall cause the fallen women to be eaten by dogs in the outskirts of the town. They are considered the greatest sinners, and not worthy of compassion."

After this visit, Ramabai began to think that there was a real difference between Hinduism and Christianity. She asked the Sisters what it was that made the Christians care for and reclaim "fallen" women. They read her the story of Christ meeting the Samaritan woman at the well and told her about the infinite love Christ had for sinners.

From that point on, Ramabai was drawn to Christianity and intellectually convinced of its truth. She felt that she had found a new religion that was better than any other religion she had known before. She was baptized and confirmed and began reading a variety of books about Christianity, but she became confused about all the sects, some of which reminded her of the various sects within Hinduism.

Ramabai was attracted to Christianity because it offered its privileges to both men and women, with no regard to class. But she still longed for something more, something she hadn't found. Eight years later she realized that she had found the Christian religion but hadn't found Christ. Looking back, she felt that there were two reasons why she hadn't had this encounter earlier. One is that she hadn't ever let go of the Hindu notion that she had to earn her own salvation. Another was that although she had read many books about the faith, she had done little reading in the Bible. So she began studying the Bible and meditating on it. As a result, she came to know Christ.

She later wrote about that time, "The Holy Spirit made it clear to me from the Word of God, that the salvation which God gives through Christ is present, and not something future. I believed it; I received it; and I was filled with joy."

Reflecting on her years as a Hindu, she wrote, "While the old Hindu scriptures have given us some beautiful precepts of loving, the New Dispensation of Christ has given us the grace to carry these principles into practice, and that makes all the difference in the world."

Ramabai went back to India, where she lived a remarkable life. She founded a home to rescue Hindu widows—women whose lives were made so miserable after the death of their husbands that they often preferred to die. She also wrote books and worked on Bible translations. And during the great famine of 1896–97, she organized food relief for the victims. Hearing of the Welsh Revival of 1904, Ramabai started prayer circles at Mukti, her center for widows and orphans, and the prayers of these young women led to a revival in India—the first of its kind.

■ ■ The Tao Became Flesh
■ ■ *Thomas In-Sing Leung*

Thomas In-Sing Leung grew up in a family that fled from the communist regime in mainland China to Hong Kong. His father's deep bitterness about the suffering he had endured eventually led to mental illness.

When Thomas witnessed this change in his father, he suffered and tried to find a teaching that would liberate him from his suffering. As a teenager he started reading Buddhist books and practicing meditation. He found that it was easier to understand "nothingness and emptiness" because he had fewer attachments to escape from than older people did.

At each level of meditation, he experienced certain realizations. At the fifth level, he discovered that the universe has creative thought or energy behind it. In Chinese philosophy, this creative energy is called the Tao, the ultimate creativity of all things. At this stage, Leung felt that he had gained a feeling of compassion and was one with the Tao.

"When I reached this level, I basically changed. I was no longer a secular person, but became more like a religious master. I encountered higher spirits that looked like angels, Buddhist avatars, or Taoist immortal persons. They offered me supernatural powers if I worshiped them. I also got into astrology and fortune-telling, because I had a power that was channeled from the spiritual world. I thought, 'Well maybe I can become a living Buddha.'"

But as a person who wanted liberation and truth, Thomas found that he had not gained real truth. With his power came a desire to control people. He had entered university and was using his fortune-telling to impress pretty girls. He began to feel that the spirits were not from God but from the devil.

Studying religion at the university, he discovered that most Buddhist immortals were not real persons in history but characters from stories. He wondered how he could have encountered them if they weren't real and decided they were evil spirits who had tricked him into believing that they were Buddhist immortals.

He rejected those spirits and gave up his supernatural powers. But he kept meditating and kept looking for God. Through meditating, he knew that behind the Tao there is the great source of creativity. There must be a Creator.

He says, "But I just could not come close to that God. I found that there was an abyss between me and God, the abyss of sin. And I knew no bridge between us. I knew that there was a God, but I could not come close to him because he was transcendent, perfect, and totally good, and I myself was limited and imperfect; I was sinful. Where was the bridge?"

Then a Christian he knew invited Thomas to a Bible study. The people in the group were loving toward him, but when they asked Thomas what he thought about the Bible, he said, "Well, the Bible has very good teaching; however, I have found the same teaching in the Hindu scriptures." He had come to the Bible study with Hindu scriptures in order to taunt the Christians. He also came with a lot of philosophical and religious questions that he felt they would be unable to answer. In fact, they weren't able to answer those questions, which pleased Thomas.

But when he returned to the Bible study, he began to feel that the Christians were really communicating with God. They were able to pray in happiness and gratitude, even when they were going through difficult times. As he watched them, he came to realize that they had discovered the way through the abyss. They had a bridge to encounter God, and that bridge was Jesus Christ.

"I discovered that Jesus Christ is the Tao. In the Chinese Bible, we use the term "Tao" to translate logos, or the "Word": 'In the beginning was the Tao . . .' Well, that's very Chinese. And then the Tao became flesh. In Chinese philosophy we don't have that, the Tao becoming flesh. But Jesus Christ is the incarnation of the Tao. He is the ultimate truth. The Tao or Logos in this regard is personal and transcendent, not just the ultimate way or principle.

"I tried really sincerely to study Christianity and found that Jesus Christ was different. He came to the earth and died on the cross and then rose from the dead. He became a bridge that can bring us to a personal relationship with God. I felt so strange, because I had such a long history of practicing meditation, but I couldn't encounter this God through it.

"The Christians had no need to practice meditation. Instead, by faith, they said 'I accept Jesus Christ,' and they could communicate with God. Only Jesus Christ said, 'I am the Way and the Truth and the Life.' Buddha didn't say that. Confucius didn't say that. They were great sages, great teachers, but they were just human beings. They couldn't bring me to God. Only Jesus Christ was able to do that."

■　　　■　　　■

All Christians affirm that Jesus Christ is God's unique revelation. But believers in diverse cultures have special insights into how that revelation is lived out. These contributions from the global church can give us new inspiration for our own faith.

Artist friends of mine who have visited Bali, where the arts have long been integrated into daily life, rave about the church services there—the way the Christian community incorporates the arts into worship in fresh and creative ways. In Australia, aboriginal people who've become Christians are creating powerful and mysterious paintings that reflect both their culture and their faith.

A few years ago I had a cross-cultural Christian experience in my own town. The Berkeley Rep hosted a South African theater company's production of a play called *Woza Albert!* This play asked what would happen if Jesus Christ came to South Africa. (This was when South Africa was still under apartheid.) In the play Jesus did return to South Africa, where he ended up in prison with other enemies of the state. But the prison couldn't hold him for long.

In the play's final scene, Jesus appears in a graveyard where, one by one, he brings a number of South African martyrs back to life, including Steve Biko and civil rights crusader Albert Luthuli ("Woza Albert!" is Sotho for "Arise Albert!"). This scene presented an electrifying and moving testimony to the gospel. The immediacy of live theater brought the meaning of the resurrection home in a new and powerful way.

Epilogue

Some years ago I was in Mexico City covering the International Women's Year Conference for *Radix* magazine and the Evangelical Press Association. As I was standing in a corridor outside one of the sessions, a little old lady with a white kerchief on her head walked by. I looked at her more closely and realized that it was Mother Teresa. I went over and told her how much I admired her work and asked for an interview. She agreed to the interview; we just had to arrange a time.

All during the week of the conference, I placed telephone calls to try to set up the interview, and finally, near the end of the week, I was able to meet with her in a hotel coffee shop in the Zona Rosa. As we were getting into the interview, an expensively dressed woman approached us and began gushing over Mother Teresa. I was very unhappy with this intrusion and also had an attitude about this society woman. But Mother Teresa was gracious and seemed to have a genuine interest in her. The woman finally left, and when we had finished the interview Mother Teresa asked whether I was a Catholic. I answered "no" but said that I was a Christian. She looked a little doubtful, the way people in the Protestant church I was raised in looked if someone said they were a Catholic Christian.

Later, when I thought about that afternoon, I realized that Mother Teresa had agreed to the interview to witness to me— she certainly didn't need the publicity a small Christian magazine could bring her. Her interest in me was the same she had for the lepers she served daily, the same she had for the woman in the coffee shop with the huge rings on her hands.

I had asked Mother Teresa to put her address on my business card so I could mail her a copy of the interview. When I looked at the card later I saw that in addition to her address she had written, "Stay close to Jesus."

It's the best advice I have ever been given, and it's the best I can offer.

—Sharon Gallagher

Notes

1   Kathleen Norris, *Dakota* (New York: Houghton Mifflin, 1993), 145–146.

2   C.S. Lewis, *Mere Christianity* (New York: Macmillan, 1943), 56.

3   Frederick Buechner, *Wishful Thinking: A Theological ABC* (San Francisco: HarperCollins, 1973), 79.

4   W.H. Auden, "For the Time Being: A Christmas Oratorio," *Collected Poems* (New York: Vintage, 1991.), 399.

5   John Otwell, *And Sarah Laughed* (Philadelphia: the Westminster Press, 1977), 191.

6   Phillip Yancey, *What's So Amazing About Grace?* (Grand Rapids: Zondervan. 1997), 64.

7   All direct quotes from Newton are taken from *But Now I See: The Life of John Newton* (Edinburgh: The Banner of Truth Trust, 1868). 25–27.

8   Peggy Alter, *Resurrection Psychology* (Chicago: Loyola University Press, 1994), 69.

9   Most of the material in this section is taken from *Cash: the Autobiography* by Johnny Cash and Patrick Carr (New York: HarperCollins, 1998).

10 Interview with Lorraine Ali, *Newsweek Online*, Nov. 2000, www.newsweek.msnbc.com.

11 Dorothy Day, *The Long Loneliness* (San Francisco: HarperCollins, 1952), 139.

12 Jacques Ellul, *The Humiliation of the Word* (Grand Rapids: Eerdmans, 1985), 47.

13 Robert Bellah, "The Recovery of Biblical Language in American Culture," *Radix* (18:4), 29.

14 Dietrich Bonhoefer, *Life Together* (San Francisco: HarperCollins, 1954), 20.

15 "Interview with Kathleen Norris," *Radix* (23:3, 1995), 11.

[16] Kathleen Norris, *Dakota* (New York: Houghton Mifflin, 1993), 98.

[17] Ibid., 146.

[18] John G. Stackhouse, in a letter to the editor, *Radix* (26:4, 1999), 30.

[19] Jaroslav Pelikan, *Jesus Through the Centuries* (New Haven: Yale University Press), 1.

[20] Stanton, Anthony and Gage, *The History of Woman Suffrage, Volume I* (Rochester, N.Y., 1881).

[21] *Narrative of Sojourner Truth* (Battle Creek, Michigan, 1878), 67.

[22] Malcolm Muggeridge, "Alternatives to Christianity," *Right On* (May 1974), 10.

[23] Ibid.

[24] "Muggeridge on Media," an interview with Steve Turner, *Right On* (May 1975), 1.

[25] William Everson: A Conversation the the Poet," interview by Sharon Gallagher and Connie Higdon, *Right On* (March 1975), 11.

[26] Quoted in Lee Bartlett's *William Everson: The Life of Brother Antoninus* (New York: New Directions, 1988).

[27] *Right On*, 5.

[28] Ibid.

[29] Dorothy Day, *The Long Loneliness* (San Francisco: HarperCollins, 1952), 24.

[30] Ibid., 84.

[31] C.S. Lewis, *Letters of C.S. Lewis* (New York: Harcourt Brace Jovanovich, 1966), 141.

[32] All other Lewis quotes are from C.S. Lewis, *Surprised by Joy* (New York: Harcourt, Brace & World, Inc., 1955), 236.

[33] Frederick Buechner, *The Sacred Journey* (San Francisco: HarperCollins, 1982), 104.

[34] Simone Weil, *Waiting for God* (New York: HarperCollins, 1951), 27.

[35] All quotes from Augustine are from *The Confessions of Saint Augustine*, translated by Edward B. Pusey (New York: Collier Books, 1972).

[36] All direct quotes from Merton are from *Seven Story Mountain* (New York: Harcourt, Brace & Co., 1948).

[37] Joy Davidman, *Smoke on the Mountain* (Philadelphia: The Westminster Press, 1953), 22.

[38] Laurel Gasque, "Christian Arts in Asia, Africa, and Latin America," Radix (23:2, 1995), 8.

[39] All direct quotes are from *Pandita Ramabai*, introduced by Shamsundar Manohar Adhav (Madras: the Christian Literature Society, 1979).

Bibliography

This is a brief list of books by some of the people whose stories were told in this book, along with some of the books mentioned as being helpful in coming to faith.

Augustine, Saint. *The Confessions of Saint Augustine.* New York: Collier Books, 1972.

Buechner, Frederick. *Wishful Thinking: A Theological ABC.* San Francisco: HarperCollins, 1973.

Buechner, Frederick. *The Sacred Journey.* San Francisco: HarperCollins, 1982.

Cash, Johnny and Carr, Patrick. *Cash: The Autobiography.* New York: HarperCollins, 1998.

Chesterton, G.K. *Everlasting Man.* San Francisco: Ignatius Press, 1993 edition.

Colson, Charles. *Born Again.* Twentieth Anniversary Edition. Grand Rapids: Fleming H. Revell, 1996.

Day, Dorothy. *The Long Loneliness.* San Francisco: HarperCollins, 1952.

Ellul, Jacques. *The Humiliation of the Word.* Grand Rapids: Eerdmans, 1985.

Johnson, Phillip E. *The Wedge of Truth: Splitting the Foundations of Naturalism.* Downers Grove, IL: InterVarsity Press, 2000.

Kempis, Thomas. *Imitation of Christ.* Nashville: Nelson Reference, 1999.

Kerr, Graham. *The Gathering Place: Informal International Menus That Bring Families Back to the Table.* Camano Press, Stanwood, WA, 1997.

Kerr, Treena. *Substance in Shadow: A Collection of Poems.* Mt. Vernon: Kerr Corp., 2001.

Lamott, Anne. *Traveling Mercies: Some Thoughts on Faith.* New York: Anchor Books, 2000.

Lewis, C.S. *Mere Christianity.* New York: Macmillan, 1943.

Lewis, C.S. *Surprised by Joy.* New York: Harcourt, Brace & World, Inc., 1975.

McDowell, Josh. *More Than a Carpenter.* Wheaton, IL: Tyndale House. 1987 edition.

McDowell, Josh. *New Evidence That Demands a Verdict.* Nashville: Nelson Reference, 1999.

Merton, Thomas. *Seven Story Mountain.* New York: Harcourt, Brace & Co., 1948.

Norris, Kathleen. *Dakota.* New York: Houghton Mifflin, 1993.

Pelikan, Jaroslav. *Jesus Through the Centuries.* New Haven: Yale University Press, 1997.

Perkins, John. *Beyond Charity: The Call to Christian Community Development.* Grand Rapids, MI: Baker Book House, 1993.

Ramabai, Pandita. *Pandita Ramabai.* (introduction by Shamsundar Manohar Adhav), Madras: the Christian Literature Society, 1979.

Schaeffer, Francis. *The God Who Is There.* 30th Anniversary Edition. Downers Grove: InterVarsity Press, 1998.

Stott, John. *Basic Christianity.* Revised Edition. Grand Rapids: Wm. B. Eerdmans, 1986.

Truth, Sojourner. *Narrative of Sojourner Truth.* Battle Creek, 1878.

Weil, Simone. *Waiting for God.* New York: Harper Collins, 1951.

Yancey, Phillip. *What's So Amazing About Grace?* Grand Rapids: Zondervan, 1997.

Organizations

(A brief list of organizations mentioned by people in the book.)

Alpha Course—www.alphausa.org

Bible Study Fellowship—www.bsfinternational.org

Billy Graham Association—www.billygraham.org

Child Evangelism—www.gospelcom.net/cef; mailing address: P.O. Box 348, Warrenton, MO 63383-0348

New College Berkeley—www.newcollegeberkeley.org

Prison Fellowship—www.pfm.org; P.O. Box 17500, Washington, DC 20041-7500

Radix magazine—www.radixmagazine.com; P.O. Box 4307, Berkeley, CA 94704

The John Perkins Foundation for Reconciliation and Development—www.jmpf.org; 1831 Robinson Street, Jackson, MS 39209

InterVarsity Christian Fellowship—www.gospelcom.net/iv; 6400 Schroeder Road, P.O. Box 7895, Madison WI 53707-7895

Wycliffe Bible Translators—www.wycliffe.org; P.O. Box 628200, Orlando, FL 32862-8200

Young Life—www.younglife.org; P.O. Box 520, Colorado Springs, CO 80901

Youth with a Mission—www.ywam.org

Credits

The following articles that originally appeared in *Radix* magazine provided source material for some of the stories: "Reflections of an Ex," by Brooks Alexander; "Alternatives to Christianity," by Malcolm Muggeridge; "A Refugee from the Haight Raps," by Mary Phillips; "Captured by the King," by Arnie Bernstein; "From Rural Mississippi and Back Again," by John Perkins; "A Gift Redeemed," by Elizabeth Claman; "The Appeal of Buddhist Spirituality," by Thomas In-Sing Leung; "William Everson: A Conversation with the Poet," by Connie Higdon and Sharon Gallagher; "Muggeridge on Media," interview by Steve Turner; "Charles Colson Interview," by David Gill and Sharon Gallagher; "Interview with Graham Kerr," by Susan Fetcho, David Fetcho, and Sharon Gallagher; "Interview with Anne Lamott," by Woody Minor and Sharon Gallagher; and interviews with Maria Muldaur, Noel Paul Stookey, Alex Mukulu, and Kathleen Norris, by Sharon Gallagher.

In a few cases, people have chosen to use pseudonyms in their stories.

All Scripture quotations, except when noted, are taken from *The Holy Bible: New Revised Standard Version,* copyright 1989, division of Christian Education of the National Council of the Churches of Christ in the United States of America, published by Oxford University Press, Inc.

About the Author

Sharon Gallagher is the editor of *Radix* magazine, "Where Christian Faith Meets Contemporary Culture." She is also associate director and professor of Christianity and Media at New College Berkeley. Her interviews, reviews, and articles appear regularly in *Radix* and have been published in many other publications, including *Eternity, Sojourners, The San Francisco Chronicle,* and *The Christian Herald.* She has published chapters in anthologies and entries in theological encyclopedias on topics including the media, ecology, and women's studies. She has also lectured in a number of colleges and seminaries on these and other topics.

Sharon lives in Berkeley, California, with her husband, Woody, an architectural historian and writer.

About the Press

"...the language of the wise brings healing."
—Proverbs 12:18b

At PageMill Press, we publish books that explore and celebrate the Christian life. Our titles cover a wide range of topics including spiritual memoir, devotional and contemplative life, peace and justice, faith-based community work, spiritual disciplines, reference works, family and parenting, spirituality, and fiction.

We believe that publishing involves a partnership between the author, publisher, bookseller, and reader. Our commitment as a publisher to this partnership is to produce wise and accessible books for thoughtful seekers across the full spectrum of the Christian tradition.

The Press seeks to honor the writer's craft by nurturing the felicitous use of language and the creative expression of ideas. We hope and believe that knowledge and wisdom will result.

For a catalogue of PageMill Press publications, for editorial submissions, or for queries to the author, please direct correspondence to:

PageMill Press
2716 Ninth Street
Berkeley, CA 94710
Ph. 510-848-3600
Fax. 510-848-1326